Whispers from Heaven

A Mother Paints Her Triumphs
and Sorrow with Words

LIZ CARTHY

BALBOA
PRESS

A DIVISION OF HAY HOUSE

Balboa Press books may be ordered through booksellers or by contacting:

Balboa Press
A Division of Hay House
1663 Liberty Drive
Bloomington, IN 47403
www.balboapress.com
1-(877) 407-4847

Because of the dynamic nature of the Internet, any web addresses or links contained in this book may have changed since publication and may no longer be valid. The views expressed in this work are solely those of the author and do not necessarily reflect the views of the publisher, and the publisher hereby disclaims any responsibility for them.

The author of this book does not dispense medical advice or prescribe the use of any technique as a form of treatment for physical, emotional, or medical problems without the advice of a physician, either directly or indirectly. The intent of the author is only to offer information of a general nature to help you in your quest for emotional and spiritual well-being. In the event you use any of the information in this book for yourself, which is your constitutional right, the author and the publisher assume no responsibility for your actions.

Any people depicted in stock imagery provided by Thinkstock are models, and such images are being used for illustrative purposes only.
Certain stock imagery © Thinkstock.

ISBN: 978-1-4525-7679-4 (sc)
ISBN: 978-1-4525-7678-7 (e)

Library of Congress Control Number: 2013911105

Printed in the United States of America.

Balboa Press rev. date: 6/17/2013

Table of Contents

Dedicated to the children and the
parents that grieve them
———◦⊰❦⊱◦———

"Whispers from Heaven" took me a long time to write because it was more about a process then writing a book and getting it done. You will see as you read how my writings changed. I feel I am a better writing now then I was in my beginning writings. I have learned a lot more about how to write, just by doing it. I left my beginning writings as I wrote them because I feel I will it will be more honest to the process of grief and people will be-able to relate to my pain and if they are a grieving parent reading my book they can feel validated in their process. I saved it to the end because I wanted to have a better perspective from which to write. If I had tried to write this in the beginning it would have been filled with a lot more pain and anger and I wouldn't have had the understanding that the passage of time would have brought me. The only words I could have written at that time would have been words like; "I just want him back! I don't care about the bigger picture I want my son back! It would have been words coming from my flesh crying out and it would have had no way to be satisfied except to become angry. In the beginning of the grieving process it is very much a raw pain. It is gut wrenching and you feel like you cannot breath. It is the kind of pain that makes you want to crawl in a bottle of booze. It is the kind of pain that makes you stay in bed and never want to come out. It is the kind of pain that unfortunately causes some parent's to op to end their pain and I totally understand their choice. I thought of it too! But for me when I thought of it, I would hear Ryan's little voice say, "No! No! Mommy you can't do that, you always taught me how to fight for my life, now you must fight for yours."

So as I write this dedication of course the first thought that comes to my mind is the children. Our children. For without them there would have been no need to write this book. I wish that were true, oh god I wish that were true. As I write I see our children in my head. I see them all laughing and playing. I see that great look of wonderment in their eyes as they look at the world around them. I see their characters and the wisdom they carry as if they were not children at all but old wise sages who came here to be our teachers. I think children who die young are really old souls come to teach us lessons. That's just my opinion. This book is first dedicated to them, for they paid the ultimate price. It was, after all their lives that were cut short. I want to thank each and every child for being the blessing they were in our lives. I want to tell them, thank you for showing us the parents what true courage is. Thank you for giving us the strength to go on after your deaths. I know for me I felt Ryan there on those days when I thought I couldn't take another breath in this world without him. Those days when it was so bad I thought I would die from the sheer pain of it. The word thank you just doesn't seem like enough. There has to be another word to express my gratefulness to them. My next thought is of the parents that have to grieve their child. This is where this dedication becomes personal and shuts out the rest of the world. It is here where we separate ourselves from the rest of the world where grief is concerned. Those that are grieving their children will understand what I am saying. There is no grief like the grief over losing your child. Nothing comes close to this kind of grief. It is here where I reach out with all my heart and say. I understand your pain. I feel it everyday and will until the day they put me in the ground. I wrote this book for us. I wrote it with the idea that I wanted the world to have an understanding that we are lucky to still be here on earth after putting our children in the ground and that, there is no getting over this kind of grief. It is more about learning to allow grief to walk next to you so you are not walking in it. That takes a lot of time and it is only in our time and not in the world's understanding of our timetable, that we make that choice. I wanted most of all to help them understand how so many of the things they say to us the grieving parent, are very painful. I wanted to be a voice for those of us that can't put it to words but need to express it. My son Ryan opened up this door for me in my writing. It was through his death that brought me to such a deep level in my writing. His death gave me the freedom to write from that very raw place. It was the pain of that place and of his death that unearthed the realness and rawness in my writing. It was his gift to me, to help me survive his death. He knew I wouldn't be able to make it unless somehow I could honor his death and not let it be in vain. He is not only my hero; he was and still is my greatest teacher.

You as a grieving parent will understand what I am going to say next. When our children died apart of us died too. I know for me I feel like a whole new person. I often wonder where Liz went. I feel like a stranger in a new world. I fight for my sanity or I should say the sanity in it. It is a strange thing to describe. I know all my parts are here. I know my mind is, because it feels so confused and I know my heart is because it is broken and as far as my soul goes it feels bruised. The thing I had the hardest time with is feeling connected to this new person. As I go on and go further down the road I never wanted to go, I realize this is how it is going to be. I just need to get comfortable with this feeling. That is the hard part for us as grieving parents. This book is really about change and choices. The change happened the second our children died. The choices will happen as we process down the road back to life. It is in this writing that I can truly be myself and let down my guard. It is with you, those of us who have lost our children to death that I can be the old me again. I can return to the place that feels familiar, the place that has Ryan in it. Where I can share about him and not make anyone feel un-comfortable by doing so. This book is in total dedication to our children and to us the grieving parent who will have to find the courage and strength to go on without them.

May God bless you in your efforts to stay alive in a world without your child? This book is for you. It is for us, the grieving parent. It is a place you can come to, to see the words that could never totally describe the pain. It is a place to come to, to find validation and fellowship in a club no one wanted to join. It is the place to come to when you want to hear the language only you can understand.

Most of my book was written in the first few years when the pain was what I was living on. It was that pain that helped to move from one day to the next. It was that pain, that made Ryan real to me and kept him close. I have now come to a different place and understanding of that pain. I have come to a place where I have learned how to let it go and still have Ryan close to me. I have kept the pain of losing Ryan in this book to allow us as grieving parents to keep it real and to validate each other. But the most important reason I wrote this book is this; I wanted to let others like myself see that you can survive the death of your child and not only survive the death but do it with the joy of living again. There will be many days when the wave of grief will engulf you and you feel like it is the beginning again or it feels that it just happen yesterday. Their will always be days like that through the process but as you go on and I can only speak from my experience but they start to happen fewer and further in between. I hope when you read this and the rest of my book, that you realize you are not alone. You are alone in your grief for your child yes, but you are not alone in the experience. We are in this together. And together we will go down that road none of us wanted to go and as we travel down that road we will realize that somewhere on that road our children took our hands and lead us back into life.

With love
Liz Weyhknecht

Foreword

Sami's words

So as I take a deep breath and reflect back to my childhood it brings me back to the remembrance of my cousin Ryan Michael Saberon, a very strong and brave young boy who didn't have the chance to follow his dreams.

Although Ryan had accomplished allot in his short life and touched many people along the way. And of course he didn't know at the age six years old how long he would live, but somehow he knew and had an understand he wasn't to live long and he wasn't going to beat cancer.

What child at that age would think like that? Children at that age are really selfish and only think about what they want. They think about school and who their friends are or going outside to play with their friends planning their next adventure and sometimes getting the occasional scrapped knee.

Ryan never got the chance to attend school and seldom went outside, because the occasional scraped knee was too risky, and dangerous a scrapped for Ryan knee could send him to the hospital for days or even weeks.

As time went by this became Ryan's new normal and missing out on childhood activities didn't seem to bring him down, I guess you can say he wasn't a child anymore, often making jokes about his sickness to bring enlightenment, and humor to others.

"Hey mom I am not growing up, I am going up," "get it" was just one of many.

So often people with illness are the ones you see with the biggest smiles and the least complaints. While we the healthy people walk around so gloomy and glum, with the most complaints. Taking no notice to life chances we have and opportunities that await us.

Sometimes we get so caught up in our own everyday living with all its pressures and demands we take life for granted, instead of taking advantage of every moment of this precious time we have here on earth, to accomplish the goals and dreams we set for ourselves and then in that same thought fully realizing there are some people who were never given that chance to see their goals met and their dreams played out on life's grand stage.

Instead I get to be stuck here with a scar on my heart from watching my cousin; my brother perishes in front of me. Things like this you can't just put a band aid on and hope it goes away. This pain isn't going away anytime soon, I am just going to have to learn to know Ryan in a different way.

Ryan battled for two years with most of his time spent in the hospital around other sick children his age or maybe even younger. He saw a few of his friends die and then seen them being wheeled right passed his room in the hospital to go to the morgue.

Throughout all of the chemotherapy, tubes, pricks, and pokes from needles, and countless surgeries, Ryan had goals and dreams. He always kept that sparkle in his eyes.

Could you imagine being so contained and limited to what you can do when everything around you feels so hopeless and still have a vision of what you would want to be when you grow up? Now that for me was inspirational, that is influence.

No matter what I will always keep my head up no matter what is going on in my life. I will wake everyday thankful for another chance to live and experience life. The most important thing Ryan has taught me and many others was to stay strong even when it seems like all hope is faded, because it can always be worse.

That could have been me on that cancer battle field watching my life unfold in front of me. Instead I got a chance, a chance to apply myself and go for my dreams. I have been influenced for the rest of my life by an eight year old little boy who in the two years he was sick never gave up the thought of a dream and he got to do that before he left this plain.

Ryan got to do allot of special things before he died. And one of those things was when the Make a Wish Foundation sent him to see The Lion King on Broadway. Ryan also got to meet his favorite actor Tom Hanks who he so loved in Forrest Grump the movie. Ryan took a beautiful picture with Tom Hanks which is hanging up on my wall that I wake up to everyday too.

For Ryan he was still just a little boy. He spent days staring out of the window at the other children in his complex as they rode their bikes. He asked his mother "Mommy why can't I ride my bike", and his mother replied "because you can get hurt Ryan" Ryan shouted "I don't care if I get hurt Mom, I just want to ride "and as time went by Ryan's mother realized maybe he wouldn't survive, so she had to make a choice.

The choice was either to allow Ryan to keep crying and begging to just be a kid and ride his bike or to take him by the hand and open the basement door and watch Ryan run to his favorite yellow bike with the biggest smile on his face saying "Mommy really, really can I ride my bike. And his mother saying really, really Ryan you can ride your bike. And with that Ryan's mom told him to ride like the wind. Ryan's mother knew she just made a choice for Ryan no matter what fears she was having she knew this could be his last ride.

Ryan rode that bike all day, and well into the night even after all the other children had given up, because there was always tomorrow to ride again for them. Finally after many hours Ryan gave in with hopes of riding again another day but unfortunately Ryan never got the chance to ride his yellow bike again.

I remember so clearly my father getting the call. I didn't know what was said to my father, but while watching the tears stream down his face, my heart dropped and I thought to myself was, that's it. My cousin was dead and gone forever. I took it very hard, even as a ten year old and now fourteen years later I am reminded of one of the biggest accomplishments Ryan made before leaving this place. His biggest dream of all was becoming a police officer. Ryan was taken down to city hall and sworn in as a Long Branch Police Officer at the age of eight. Ryan was given a badge number twenty two and a uniform perfect to the fit.

I think to myself there's nothing I can't do if only I push myself. It was Ryan that taught me that. I have been given a chance to reach my goals. I have been given a chance at life. Ryan has influenced me to strive and never give up because he has done things in a short time that not allot of people get to do in a lifetime. So I now know I will take my chances I will go for my goals no matter what while always remembering in my heart that little boy in blue, my cousin, my big brother Ryan riding his bike off into the sunset taking a little piece of me to heaven with him

Preface

Whispers from Heaven

Whispers from heaven, is my story of dealing with the grief over losing my little boy Ryan to cancer. The book gives you opportunity to walk with me on a daily basis and feel some of the pitfalls and landmines waiting around every corner.

Just when you think you are doing well and the day seems bright, a school bus stops right in front of you and lets out the neighborhood kids Ryan went to school with. My book allows you the opportunity to see the bigger picture but also honors the feelings you may be feeling at any given moment. The moments when anger comes in and you just want to scream at the school bus and tell it to go away.

In this book it lets you into a sacred place, a very private place, where only thoughts of your child are allowed in. It is in this place that the real lessons of life are found if we the grieving parents are willing to share in this place and let others in to see our pain and experience it through our words without having to pay the ultimate price we were made too.

My wish is for those souls brave enough to go there with us and share in our pain so they will come out with a better understanding for: 1) who their children are in their lives and what previous gifts they are and hopefully treat them as such. 2) To give them a better understanding for those of us who have lost our children to death and how this death cannot be compared to any other death. It has a lot to do with how the things people say can be very painful and it speaks of how it is sometimes better to say nothing at all and just be there for support. We as grieving parents understand the need to want to say something; after all we were once a non-grieving parent ourselves.

That's why I felt the need to share. I figured that if I have to be here why not make the best of it and draw a bridge between the two worlds and by doing that, I could at least honor my sons death in some way and not be swallowed up by the grief over losing him and thirdly: To valid those parents who cannot put their feelings to words. To let them know, I understand them and although their grief is different than mine and we share the same experience of losing a child to death and we belong to a club no one wanted to join and to let them know, I too have crazy thoughts, Like; wanting to go to the cemetery with a backhoe and dig Ryan up, bring him home, put a blanket on him and just stare at him because dead is better then nothing. I share about the times I want to scream out loud "would someone please mention his name and make him real and not act like he didn't exist please!"

In this book I am willing to open up my heart and soul because I feel Ryan and I made a pact along time ago, way before we both came here and now I am going to honor that pact no matter how painful. I may not have the full picture now but I know someday I will. So until then I will continue to honor Ryan and let him know his mom is doing the best she can on this side of heaven.

The Grieving Process

The grieving process for a lack of a better way to describe one of the most painful passages of life! It is exactly that, a process. This process starts at the time-of-death. The grieving process is a never-ending motion of the ups and the downs and a whole-lot of in-between for the person, who is grieving and it will affect every aspect of their lives, including all those around them, it will require allot of understanding, love and support for the grieving person. For most grieving people, the idea of going through stages is something they find hard to except. The reason being is just this; they do not want to be placed, into a category or lumped together with everyone else. Grief is so very personal and although you may share the same type of grief it is still a very personal and private matter for each person who grieves. It is more about their relationship with the person who has died that makes it different. The person grieving does not want to be-placed into a cookie cutter mentality of the stages of grief. They want to feel the process in their own special way. The person grieving wants to know, that it is okay to be wherever, they are in the process. They need to know that they are not crazy for having so called, crazy thoughts about themselves or the person they are grieving. Depending on the type of death and who it is to them, the process is very different, for those who have lost their children, this kind of grieving is one of the most painful processes through grief. This is one of the hardest for the one grieving and for all those around them. Having been through this one myself, I can say I have experienced many deaths in my life including my eight year old sister and my father and none could compare with the death of my eight-year old son Ryan to cancer. His death requires every ounce of my strength on a daily bases, to go on as I process through my grief. There is a line in the book I wrote, that talks about being stuck in grief or as I put it, walking in grief. In my book it gives the reader an alternative, to just walking in grief and that alternative is to allow grief to walk next to them instead. The benefit from allowing grief to walk next to them is this: Grief becomes like a shadow and just like your shadow follows you around so too does grief. As your shadow does, it never hinders your walk because it never gets in the way. It moves with you not behind you or ahead of you but with you. It never stops your forward motion; it is just there to be that subtle reminder that it exists and it will not go away, it will just find its place in your everyday living. Grief and the whole process of grief is a scary subject to most people. Who wants to talk about death and the dying process? Unfortunately, this is not being realistic because death is all around us and even more so in these Times, when no matter where you turn you hear about people dying. Sooner or Later death touches us all and there is going to be no getting around it. Grief is here to stay so why not try to have an understanding for the Process. If not for yourself, why not for someone else, because you never know when you may need to have someone understand your process as you go through grief when it happens to you.

The hope of tomorrow

When I first started writing my feelings down I was doing just for me. I felt like if I didn't get this pain out of me, I was going to just die from the brutal pain of it. Writing after writing I tried to express to myself this terrible pain that was consuming my life. Before my son Ryan's death I was always the kind of person who chooses to always see the hope in tomorrow. I was always that kind of person. In the very beginning of my grief journey when I was living and breathing the pain to the point I couldn't even catch my breath and the tomorrows came and I did not even know it. And to tell you the truth I did not want to know it, or care to know it but tomorrow has a funny way of doing that. I hated tomorrows and wanted no part of them. And all I wanted to do was to stay in the pain of losing my child. Well I am happy to admit I no longer see it that way at all. I love tomorrows now and I can actually feel the joy tomorrow brings. This feeling did not happen overnight and it was a long road to get to this place called tomorrow. I do not know if it will happen for you? I do know this, it can happen. And when it does happen, it will be in the way you choose to view it and that my friend is for every person to make the choice. And after a few years of writing down my feelings I realize I was actually writing a book of my pain and sorrow over the death of my son Ryan. Whenever I went to go buy a book to try to see myself in it I had a hard time finding the one that said it just right for me. So I wrote the book that I wanted to read. The kind of book that said it and it said it without prettying it up with fancy words to make it more palatable for the world to see. I just wanted to write a book I would read. I wanted my book to be real and to express the many different sides of grief. And in doing that express the many different sides allowing everyone who is grieving a child to find their self-validation no matter where they choose to be in that process.

There is no special formula or potion. It can come in the smallest of thoughts or even in the whisper of your child. It can be found in an old man eyes or the simple touch of a hand. It can be seen in a smile you found in your mirror as you quickly looked away and the reasons our as different as we are from each other. My hope is that you find yourself a reason and lend a helping hand and by doing that you will truly honor your child and help yourself in the process. May God bless all grieving parents and hold them close. And know my thoughts are with you all as we journey this path in life and until we can be with our children again.

With Love and hugs
Liz

The pain of Ryan section A

A Different Ryan

Through the cloud of days just after we found out that Ryan had cancer, I was in the pre-op room with him. I was rubbing his back and just trying to comfort him in any little way possible. I wanted to comfort him like; I had done so many times before since he was a baby. I wanted so much to take that cancer right out of him! We were still in a state of shock. So as I was saying I was rubbing Ryan's back. When out of nowhere he says to me, do not worry the old Ryan is gone, but the new one is here. Till this day I still don't know what he meant.

Ryan always said such profound things, and it was just the beginning. My life was in a whirlwind and still is. I can still see the faces of all the people involved, the look in their eyes when they were treating Ryan. I didn't like what I saw in them, they looked sad. However, I just would not let that affect me. I couldn't because I would just fall to piece' if I did. I went through each day taking on the task of that day only.

It is hard to explain what takes over, it has to be something outside of you, and I prefer to call it God. I used to think in pretty black and white terms when it came to God, not anymore. I'm still processing all of that now. In the beginning I think I closed out God. Not consciously, but just because my mind couldn't accept what was going on, and therefore it couldn't accept him. I didn't have the understanding or the means to understand. I'm trying to look at it in that bigger way. I think I am making some headway. Sometimes I think I can actually see some light at the end of the tunnel. Never thought I would ever hear myself say that. I couldn't imagine in my wildest dreams ever seeing any light again. Somehow it is seeping back into my life. How dare you life, sneak back into my life when I do not want you too. How dare you life! How dare you go on without Ryan in it. I think this is what bothers me the most and is the hardest thing about moving on.

A Letter from Grief

I came here with no language yet all people and all lands know me. I wreak havoc with your mind and body. I play nasty head games. I can take a beautiful day and put it to ruins. There is no way to escape me when I come. I make myself invisible. I become loud and present to only the one I come and visit, and they have to walk in the world as if I am not there. I am a scrapbook ready to be opened. I am an unwanted visitor. I came to unearth the volcano deep inside your core. I dig, and dig, day after day. I bring up piece after piece of fragments of your pain and anger and disbelief of what has happened to you. I like being in control of your every emotion. I live for this! I am alive in this! I put a lot of trust in your memory to help my cause and as usual I have no problem there. Thank you for that. In the beginning, my job is so very easy. I usually get no resistance. I move around at will causing deep valleys of sorrow and pain. I can talk you into anything I want. I tell you things such as; life is not worth living go-ahead let go and die.

If you want to get away from me, I will show you how. It really is not hard at all. When I come to visit, I become a master builder. I build a wall so tall and strong it would take an army to knock it down. I do a lot of my work at night. I instill pictures in your dream life. I make them haunting pictures that are very descriptive and full of sounds and smells of the moment. I have very clever and deceptive and will go to any means to invoke the rawest, of your emotions. I can take the sweetest dream and turn it into your worst nightmare. You must be saying to yourself why? Why would I do such a terrible thing to someone? Why would you get such pleasure out of someone else's pain? I do not blame you for thinking that. What else would you think? Actually, I am doing my job. The job no one else wants to do. It is like being the undertaker. Not too many people want that job but thank God, someone does it. My job is to get you to work even if you do not want me to. I am here to make you work the process of grieving. Moreover do not fool yourself; it is work, hard work and when it comes to this kind of work it can only be done by you. The work is painful and in the end can be rewarding but you will never know that until you do it. In addition, as you work through the process, you may even find that you are starting to like me. I know we could never become close friends; I bring too much pain for that, but a friend you can appreciate for the resolve I bring into your life. This is an on-going job with no end in sight. It is just moments of release from the pain and sorrow.

As you go on with the process you will notice that a lot of the unrelenting pain, and pictures, and bad dreams will give way to softer memories of smiles and whispers and eyes of love. And you will let go of the bad thoughts. So if you would not mind letting me stay awhile longer, I would love to help you down the road a little more, and I promise I will leave when the going gets too tough, and come back when you need me. I will know when that is. I have been doing this for many years now. So, keep up the good work and do not be afraid of the pain. The pain is just a reminder of the work you are doing, and from where I stand, you have done good work.

Your friend,
Grief

Dear Mommy,

know you are having a hard time adjusting to me not being there. I just want you to know I am more there now then, I have ever have been. It is like you are driving a stick shift mommy and you are in first gear and I am in second gear. It is just a matter of shifting gears that is all it is. I am traveling alongside you but I am just in a different gear now. In time you will learn to shift gears and be with me. Just try and stay in this moment I will be there with you. Do not think about it or try to figure it out. Just do it. Be in the moment. You are in kindergarten now learning a new language and soon you will be able to communicate fluently. Everything you are going through is for a reason and that reason is really only known to you, because it is you who is going through it and someday you will have the full understanding. The place you are at is not timeless as it is for me. It has boundaries. It is finite. My dying was just an advent in that space you call time. Mom, how do you measure time? Can time truly be measured? Man has a fixed seconds hour, days, weeks, months and years to time.

I will always be in your life. People believe someone is born so therefore life has begun and when they die it has just ended. How could I ever be apart from you when I am in your every thought? Therefore I am so alive. I am alive in the truest sense of the word. That is why you do not have a desire to go to my grave. You know why. Because you know I am not there.

I am energy now mom. I am just moving faster then you and because of that speed you cannot see me. My energy is not bound by flesh and blood or bone. It has liberty to move at its own will. All I have to do is think the thought and I am there.

Mom can you see how much a part of me you are? This is you writing and yet it is me. This is true because you are me, and I am you. We are separate yet we very much one and the same. You have just willed your will to step aside for me for a moment. Mom can you see now, I can become part and all of you? This understanding has always been there. You have just recognized it for the first time.

It is just matter without substance. Before matter becomes matter it has to first be thought. You will know this is me mom because you will hear the truth in it. The very sense it is making. You will not be able to deny the feeling you get inside your very core. The problem is that this now flies against all you knew to be your truth before. The truth, is the truth until a higher truth be known.

Think of it this way mom, when I was on earth I knew your voice in a crowd. I knew that voice because I grew up with it. It was familiar to me. So it is too with what I am saying to you. You know me, my voice my personality, my way of thinking.

Remember those times when you just looked at me and I did not say a word? I heard you. Just like your hearing me now. You are hearing me thought to thought. The personality is like a fingerprint in the spiritual realm. Mom let me explain to you what it is like. Let me tell you about death and heaven. I really do not like to use the word death. It sounds so final because for you

Death was so final concerning me. However, in reality it is transition. We are just like a baby when it goes into transition before it is born so we to go into transition before we die. We start to speed up our vibrations before we transcend this time and space. Some of this will be hard to understand. Take your time. Heaven is everything you said it would be and more. Remember when we talked about heaven and I would ask you all those questions?

You told me, Ryan if I would go to a book with the most beautiful pictures of earth in it and pick the prettiest you said heaven is like that but a hundred times more beautiful. And thank you mom for believing, It kept me strong and not afraid of dying. Live life to the fullest, smile, love and be loved. That is most important. I am in the greatest place anyone could want to be. No more cancer here. It is now all about warm and soft and beautiful things. I miss you Mom! I miss your big hugs and kisses and your crazy way of being. I want you to know I am truly with you. You will learn more as you go along just how much I am with you.

Love eternally
Ryan

Angels of mercy

he last three months of Ryan's life, I was hoping for a miracle for Ryan. I was waiting for a miracle that would save his life and cure him of cancer. I would spend each day with my body and mind in a fighting stance. I was ready to fend off anyone who had a negative attitude. I was committed to only allowing positive vibrations in Ryan's room.

Ryan's nurses loved him very much. I think the reason being was because he was so willing to help them to help him. Ryan very seldom complained about anything they had to do to him. Ryan thought his nurses were the greatest. I remember not long before he died someone asked him if he had a wish. He said yes I have a wish and they in return asked Ryan what it was? In addition, without hesitation Ryan said he wished he could win fifty-thousand-dollars. When Ryan was asked what would he do with the money? Ryan answered, "I would give it to all my nurses, and all the nurses in the world. I could not believe that, but then again I could when it came to Ryan. Ryan knew what his nurses meant to him. He knew he was receiving the best care in the world and he wanted the nurses to know it too.

The nurses would often come in on their days off to visit Ryan and bring special things he asked for. My angels would even call me when they were home. They still do

Moreover, it has been three months since Ryan has died. We have made lifetime friendships with some of Ryan's nurses that nothing can sever. I can't even count the number of times I cried with them, nor the times we had just as many laughs. At night when Ryan was asleep, the desk became a social event for me. I had many of my discussions on Ryan's care at the desk. I trusted Ryan's nurses like no others, not even some of the doctors! They were all for us and I knew it and most of all Ryan knew it! I would even take part in one of the highlights of the night, the ordering of the food with the staff. After three months, it felt more like home to me.

When it got down to the worst days of my life, I thank God for my nurses, because they knew me so well, that even when I felt I wasn't there in my mind they knew what to say or not to say, It took a little more than two weeks for Ryan to pass. For as usual Ryan did things his way. The night Ryan passed (Sunday Oct. 25th 1998 at 5:55 in the evening) all the nurses asked to be called. The nurses had a hotline set up so all would-be called at the appropriate time. This list was endless. In fact, people from all over the hospital in all different departments were on the list. One by one, they came in to say their good-byes to their buddy Ryan. Better known as the KING. They came from all different walks of life, but to the same place for Ryan. There were no differences when it came to Ryan's care because they all cared.

So, to my beautiful angel's how can this mother tell you how much she loves you, and always will? You will forever be a part of my life, I will think back to those moments and feel once again the love and care you had for Ryan and me. And so my Angels, I let you go to care for all the other children waiting for your love, mercy, and the special moments waiting just for them. Bye my sweets. Letting go is so, so hard but I must. Good-bye my eternal friends and thank you for being there for my little boy Ryan

Drowning in the Sea of Yesterday's

Oh God I feel like I am drowning today. I am drowning in the sea of yesterday. I have so many reminders of you. How can I ever escape the pain of losing you? Where can I hide from my thoughts? Where can I ever feel human again? Where can I ever lay back and relax my mind and body? Where can I ever go to find that place of real contentment? You know the one that comes at the end of a day when you set a goal and achieved it? You know the one I am talking about the one that has that great feeling of accomplishment? What will I ever feel accomplished about? Will I feel accomplished when I have learned to live one more day without you in it? How many years will I have to go down this road without you? That to me does not feel like an accomplishment, it feels more like something I was forced to do dragging my feet all the way. Since your death every word it subject to great scrutiny. The meanings of words as I knew them have come under a new light, and a microscope. I can never take words lightly again! This is how my world has changed. Nothing is simple anymore! I hear the words differently. People say I hope you can find some peace of mind and I cannot ever imagine finding some peace of mind. I am so lost in my world of pain I cannot find a person, a place, a thing that could give me peace of mind. I write about words. I take them and cut them up into small pieces. I see in that process how ridiculous words really are. They can never do it justice. Words are just an expression of a feeling not the feeling itself. It is the outside covering of an emotion that is intangible. I wish I could paint, or sing, or act out how this feels so the rest of the world could understand how this feels. It feels like you are in a never-ending play. To end the play is to say it is over, or it is finished. In this play there are no endings just new beginnings. In this play, you have the lead role, everything revolves around you. If you lose your place, everyone else loses theirs too. Like the actor on stage you too feel like everyone is watching your every move. What does act mean after all? To me it means to put on, or pretend, to be something or someone else and make it look good or real to the one viewing the play. It means to take them away from their real life and bring them to yours. Make it believable to them. To sweep them away with the emotion you have created on stage. Sometimes I fear this is what my life is going to be about. One long scene one after another, day in and day out. And I do not know how long anyone can keep that up. I struggle every day to get up for task of the role. I keep thinking that eventually it will become real and then I can enjoy the fruits of my labor and be proud of the job I did. I just want to feel real again and talk, and walk naturally with ease without feeling strange like I do not fit. I just want to once again belong, to feel community, to feel part of the world and not separate from it. Today is one of those days I find that hard to do. Maybe if I hold on tomorrow will be that day for me. If there is a tomorrow for me I can only hope.

I am holding myself

Today as I sit here to write, it is a Saturday and for me this Saturday left behind one of the worst Fridays I ever experienced. It was for sure my Black Friday. I am fourteen months, and nine days down the road I never wanted to walk. A road so filled with potholes, and detours and most of all roadblocks to my sanity. As I walk down this road, what I notice most is how the other people on the road are moving so quickly and seem not to be hindered at all. I feel like I am crawling in comparison. Everything to me feels like slow motion. I get the overwhelming feeling that I am invisible to them. It is such a lonely road and I get the urge to sit in the middle of the traffic just to see if it would stop and take notice.

When this feeling hits, it is so powerful it paralyzes you and freezes you right in your tracks. When a child dies, this death can't be compared to any other. I have had my father die, and my sister at age eight, and aunts, and uncles and cousins. This just doesn't come anywhere near the pain of losing a child. Nowhere near at all. I am not always in that black Friday days. Yes there are days when you wake up and the weight of the world isn't on your shoulders and you wonder why? Why is this day so different than the others? Why today can, I live with the pain of losing Ryan. I don't have the answer for that question except to say there could be no way you could be in that pain and go on living. It has to be God on those days taking our pain. I don't know the answer I really don't.

My feelings go from the lowest valley to the highest of high mountaintops and I cannot explain how I got to either one. When I take time to really ponder the process, the only explanation I feel deep down is it is grief at work walking us through our worst nightmare holding our hands in the darkest regions of our souls and trying to be our light in a very dark place. And we as parents are trying to make sense of the senseless. Trying to find a way to go on living and not feel guilty. Trying to find a way too once again let joy back in our lives. Trying to let the joy of living that we had through our children we must somehow find through ourselves. Too once again let love back into a heart that has shut down and boarded itself up. To once again let true laughter and genuine feeling be apart of our lives. Too once again see the sun as the beginning of a new day, not as our enemy that brings us one more day without our child in it. I don't know how I'm going to do this anymore then you, but somehow I have managed to be here to write this and I'm one more day down that road I didn't want to go. I am one more day down the road that never ends. The road that has many people just like me, but I did not notice because they are invisible too.

I truly feel, for a lack of a better way to describe it, as if I am holding myself because I am the one who has to get me through. I'm the one who has to get up every morning to a world without Ryan and somehow find the strength to go on. I have to find comfort in my own mind where all my remembrances and pictures of Ryan are. Starting a new day is the hardest time of the day for me. It is in that place, for a split second you forget he isn't here. You can think for a moment he is still asleep but like a wave it starts to come over you and engulf you with the reality of your day and he isn't in it. I truly am holding myself because it takes all my energy to hold myself together and live from moment to moment. I hold myself when no one is around and you feel like screaming and throwing yourself on the floor so you can die right there on the spot. It is in those times you see just how alone you are. No one can be with you every minute of the day they have their own lives to live.

I feel like I'm holding myself when I write down all my feelings. It is my way of comforting me and soothing my wound with a medicated cream or ointment. It is my way of caressing me through a very painful place when no one else is around to give me a much needed hug. So I hug myself through my words. It is through this holding and hugging process that I find the freedom to be me, plain and simple, just me. The person without her makeup, without her hair combed. The person with all her flaws and battle scars that life has left and to see the sadness and emptiness of a person lost in a world without meaning a person so lost in a world no one understands except those who have lost a child. This is why I feel like I am truly holding myself. I am holding myself in many ways. I am holding UP, holding ON, holding IN, holding OUT, but most of all I am holding the most important thing: Me.

Intimate Times

There are so many things I want to write down. I hope I can first remember them all and second I hope I can do them justice. As Ryan's mom, I shared very intimate times with Ryan when he was in the hospital. In my writings I want to capture the feeling as close as I can with just words, this is going to be very hard to do. Ryan had a way of always running the show from beginning to the end. He always had everyone around him wrapped around his finger including me. You could not know Ryan and not know this about him. He just had it that way when it came to people. You could never trap him in anything! I will give you an example. If you were to ask Ryan, Ryan, who is your favorite nurse? His answer would always be. I love them all the same. Even if he had a favorite and I know for a fact he did, he just would not hurt any of the nurse's feelings. I loved that about Ryan. Before Ryan got so sick, he could not get out of bed anymore he stayed out of his room as much as he could. He lived at the desk talking to his nurses and doctors most of the day and night. I knew Ryan was getting very sick when he no longer could go to the desk. Going there was all he wanted to do. I remember about three weeks or maybe a month before Ryan died he asked me one of the hardest questions I ever had to answer. He asked if he would be home for Christmas. I had to bite my tongue not to cry in front of him and say we are going to try as hard as we can to get you home Ryan. I knew in my heart that he was not going to make it home. That to this day still haunts me. One night just when Ryan received his nighttime medication, he asked me to help him to lie down. While I was helping him, he said mom! When I grow up will I always be this crazy in my head. I said oh no Ryan it is just the medicine do not worry. Now you just go to sleep now, okay, because mommy is here. I will always be here. Then he said something to me I will never forget. He said, mom, I just want you to know one thing, Okay! And I of course replied what is that Ryan. He said I want you to know I always want to live with you and stay with you because you always taught me how to treat people nice. With that I went out of the room into the darkened hallway looked up at God and said, and you want me to give up that! Why, are you doing this to me! God! I cannot take anymore please! Soon I heard God's voice in my heart say to me: that is a gift I gave you. Listen to what Ryan said. He said I heard you mom when you said it was not right to talk about people no matter if they are black or white or if they are gay or if they are fat people or ugly people, he said he heard you. That was such a beautiful gift he was giving you. How many other mothers do you know get that kind of gift?

Learning to Live Again

How do you tell a mom it is okay to go on living, when everything inside her is dying? How do you tell her that when all her hopes, and all her dreams, and all her wishes are buried with that child! When everything she thinks about is lying in a grave and the very picture of that is forever, imprinted and burned into her head. How would you expect her to go on?

The very act of going on means leaving her child behind, although some would say that is not true because you can still have your child, you just will have your child in a different way. Your child is still with you! I can understand that in my mind very easily, but my flesh just will not buy it! It is my flesh, which questions where are you? And wants to know why, why can't I feel you, or why can't I smell you? On the other hand, I do not understand why I cannot look into your beautiful eyes anymore? I want to know on the other hand, why, can't I hear you call me mommy?

There was a time when I too wanted to die; the pain was so bad (and sometimes still is) that all I could think about was how I wanted to be with you. When I think about that sometimes I get great comfort just going there with you. I know everyone worries when they hear me say that, but it is the truth. I can't even begin to tell you about the Pain. So now what do I do?

When I start to feel life inching its way back into that very painful place at first if I am caught off guard I fall right back into it like I never left it. Then quickly my mind reminds me of you and the fact that you are gone. Pictures flood my mind. I see you saying things and making familiar gestures with your hand and somehow wherever I'm at or whatever I'm doing just doesn't feel right anymore. So how do I get to that place where I can once again live life and enjoy it without feeling guilty? Guilty because you should be here having fun and enjoying your life like every other child is.

I guess it comes down to this. You shouldn't have died. You shouldn't have had cancer. You shouldn't have left me with this terrible pain. I know it is not your fault. However, I am still here without you to go on with life. All I can say for now is I'm doing the best I can today. There can be no tomorrows for me. There can only be today's. Today I know I can do it. However, Tomorrow will have to take care of itself and just maybe I will find myself there, in tomorrow that is.

My feelings my Thoughts

*often find myself having trouble explaining my feelings concerning my grief and what it means to me about Ryan's death. I always find myself at a loss for words. I do not know why I feel such a need to convey what this feels like! It could be, because I feel so confused most of the time about Ryan death. Moreover, what his death has it done to me?

Questions like, Who, am I? What am I? I feel like many people, different yet all one. All connected yet separate. I can see them all and understand them and how they feel. Some are angry, and justifiably so. Some of them are sad and lonely. Some are hidden deep down and afraid to come up to the surface. It would be too much trouble to explain, and they would be better off to stay hidden.

I can feel all these things happening to me. I can feel my mood changing. I know when this is happening but I just cannot stop it. Don't know if I would if I could. How do I tell someone how this feels? How can you tell someone and make him or her understand? I guest the best way to describe it is to say how can you describe color to a blind man. You yourself have seen the rainbow and you know how beautiful it is and yet, you cannot share it or describe to him, how frustrating that can be. You yourself have seen a sunset or sunrise and cannot experience it with him. Better yet, there is the other side of that which is the dark side. It would be, what I would call, the not too pretty sides of color that leaves you empty and sad. I think what I am really looking for is some kind of understanding for me. I think if I can achieve that understanding then somehow I will be-able to go on in this world. I need to know who I am! And, who I was! and who I will become after such a devastating event in my life.

Most people have that understanding throughout their life. I have always struggled with this one. I was never sure about who I am because I felt like more then one. What made me more confused was how strong I felt about who I was at the time. I was always very strong in my character. So why would I doubt? I always felt like I had a good mind and I had a good understanding of me and yet there would be times I felt weak in my mind. How can I know me, when I cannot understand who I am?

This is why I feel the need to explain what this feels like. It feels like it is crazy and it is sad and it is happy and it is angry, and it is lost and it is found. It is unimportant. It is very important. It is every emotion all at once and yet separates. It is beginnings, and it is endings, and it is UPS, and it is downs just wanting to know in all of this confusion, is there a person? Is there a person that is all together and yet not separate? Is there a person that does not feel strange but feels at home with herself? Is this person comfortable with herself? Is this person at peace and not doubting who she is? Is she proud of herself? Does this person have any doubts? Does this person have to ask for approval or permission? Is she confident in herself? This is what I want understood and recognized without asking! This is the person! That can stand there and tell you just how she is feeling. This is the person! I have always wanted to be! This is the person! I hope to become.

I guess what I'm saying is, can you see who this is? Can you accept who I am? I know this sounds like a lot of crazy talk but it is really important to me. You would have to be in me to understand that. I want to express all that I am but when I do, I hear many different voices talking in my head as if everyone is talking at once and I try to the best of my ability to sort it out and then bring it out.

I cannot believe I am trying to put this down on paper, and I am trying to make some kind of sense of it. When I try to put my feelings down on paper, I feel a rush of emotions. It is as if a wave comes over me.

When this happens I will see this little girl and she will look so lost and scared. I'll see her look around as to say where am I? Or where is everybody? Then quickly I will think of something else, or see pictures of Ryan, or hear him talk to me.

If you think, this is confusing to you just think of how it is like for me. Sometimes or I should say almost all the time, I say to myself do not share these feelings, it does=t make sense. If, I start to share, I hear myself say; what is that? What you just said, do you think anyone wants to hear that or cares what that means? So what if that is the way you feel. Keep it to yourself. No one wants to hear all that crazy stuff. I fight with myself to talk and sometimes it takes allot of energy. With all this, I am still grieving for Ryan. Ryan is right there in the middle of all this trying to find a place. He is trying to find a place to fit and belong. I can hear him saying did you forget about me? I am still here and I am not going anywhere. The reason I feel so bad is because, he should be the only person I am thinking of. He is always there because I sense him and feel him but not in the way, you would expect me to. It is as if you know it in your head but cannot feel it because someone gave you a pill that numbed you. I do not like that feeling because I know it. I knew that, that is what was happening and I did not have any control over it. Who gave them the right to take away my feelings? I decided to write because I know that no one can stop my train of thought and I have to say exactly what I feel even if it does not make any sense. I have to get it out somehow. I told myself before I started to write this. I told myself to go ahead and write it down, all it is, words on a piece of paper and words cannot hurt you. They are just words after all. In addition, it cannot hurt because just maybe someone can make some sense of all the talk. If not, that is all right too. Therefore, what I have decided to do is to start writing down my feeling more often. No matter what they sound like, they are still my feeling and a feeling is a feeling and it does not always have to make sense. At least that is what I have been told on many an occasion.

Sometimes I feel like I am in a maze. Running to find out where I am! When I first start out it is not too bad because I am thinking to myself this is not too bad, I can do this. Therefore, I go along content in my thoughts and somewhat at peace with myself. Then on certain days, it becomes scary and dark and lonely. I guess my imagination takes over and depending how I feel that day is the way I will experience the maze. I know in myself that I am moving. I feel the movement. However, I have lost my way. I know if I were able to rise about the maze I could see my way so clear through every little turn. But I don't have that advantage. I have to feel my way around like a blind man. One advantage the blind man has over me is he has been blind and being blind he has learned how to walk in his blindness. The dark isn't scary to him. He uses his other senses to help him find his way. I guess I will have to become like the blind man and learn how to use my other senses to help me through the maze. There are days when I'm in that maze when I can feel my heart racing and pounding so hard I think I will lose my breath. There are other days when I feel confident I will find my way out and I'm not scared at all. Those are the days I feel like I could climb a mountain and still have energy to go on. While all of this is happening to me remember, my outside life is still going on. I have an inside life and an outside life. We all do I believe. At least that is the way it is for me. I think when my inside life is happening that is the time I want to be alone with no intrusions. I feel good when I am there. I become almost angry when people invade that place, and break the silence and the sacredness of that place. I can go in and out of there at will when I choose to do so. I want to be the one to make the choice. When I started to write my feelings, my true feelings, I started to notice some things about myself that I had=t notice before. I feel some relief and not as frustrated as I was before I started to write. It seems that forming these thoughts that I thought couldn't be formed gives me a feeling of self. No matter how confusing it may sound to anyone else, it gave me my voice and I put it out there and it is not just a thought flying around in my head banging against the wall of my mind anymore and making me think as if I were crazy. As I write this, even now I'm saying to myself who is this person who is writing? They make a lot of sense. It can't be I. I sound so together and I say it just right. I'm looking at her and I see myself as if I were a child looking up at her. I want to grab her hand she seems so nice and smart. She is someone I want to become. And I wanted to get to know her. When I am looking at her as that child, I can sense Ryan standing there with me almost as if he was I. The two children seem to be best friends. And they are always whispering cute things into each other ears.

Why does that little girl seem so important to me? She seems so trusting and wide-eyed. When I think of her or see her in my mind, she always looks so lost. She looks as if she is looking for someone. How did she get there? Does everyone have a child they can see or hear?

When this starts happening in my writing I want to stop because I know how this must sound to others and my logical mind does not want to hear it. And everything inside of me wants to keep going. It feels so good to talk. Therefore, I am going to keep writing as if no one would ever see my writings so I can feel safe to say anything I want.

If I could talk to her, I would ask her about herself. I would ask her if she needed to tell me something or say something to me.

I can barely hear her little voice. She told me I was not crazy and that she sees me too. She says I'm very strong and she likes that about me, and plays with me a lot. She thinks I have a great sense of humor and hears me laughing a lot. She says we are no different then the rest of the world. If there is a difference it is, we just listen more than they do. We pay attention to our feelings more than most. We see far beyond what most people would even dare to dream. She says the reason she looks so sad is that she misses Ryan a lot. Ryan helped her not be so lonely. She doesn't know whether he could see her, but she thinks he did. Or just enjoyed her through me. She seems quite smart for a kid, don't you think? When I'm writing, I get this great sense of freedom I could write forever. I feel joy right now as I write. What freedom. If I could go on saying whatever I feel without the fear of someone making something out of it.

My feelings, My Thoughts I often find myself having trouble explaining my feelings concerning my grief and what it means to me about Ryan's death. I always find myself at a loss for words. I do not know why I feel such a need to convey what this feels like! Maybe it's because I feel so confused most of the time about Ryan death. Moreover, what his death has it done to me? Questions like who am I? What am I? I feel like many people. All of them different yet all one but yet connected yet separate. I can see them all and understand them and how they feel. Some are angry, and justifiably so. Some of them are sad and lonely. Some are hidden deep down and afraid to come up to the surface. It would be too much trouble to explain, and they would be better off to stay hidden. I can feel all these things happening to me. I can feel my mood changing. I know when this is happening but I just cannot stop it. Don't know if I would if I could. How do I tell someone how this feels? How can you tell someone and make him or her understand? I guess the best way to describe it is to say how you can describe color to a blind man. You yourself have seen the rainbow and you know how beautiful it is and yet, you cannot share it or describe to him, how frustrating that can be. You yourself have seen a sunset or sunrise and cannot experience it with him. Better yet, there is the other side of that which is the dark side. What I would call the not too pretty sides of color, the kind that leaves you empty and sad. I think what I am really looking for is some kind of understanding for me. I think if I can achieve that understanding then somehow I will be-able to go on in this world. I need to know who I am! And, who I was! And who I will now become after such a devastating event in my life? Most people have that understanding throughout their life. I have always struggled with this one. I was never sure about who I was because I felt like more than one. What made me more confused was how strong I felt about who I was at the time. I was always very strong in my character. So why would I doubt? I always felt like I had a good mind and I had a good understanding of me and yet there would be times I felt weak in my mind. How can I know me, when I cannot understand who I am? This is why I feel the need to explain what this feels like. It feels like it is crazy and it is sad and it is happy and it is angry, and it is lost and it is found. It is unimportant. It is very important. It is every emotion all at once and yet separate. It is beginnings, and it is endings, and it is ups, and it is downs just want to know in all of this confusion, is there a person? Is there a person that is all together and yet not separate? Is there a person that does not feel strange but feels at home with herself? Is this person comfortable with herself? Is this person at peace and not doubting who she is? Is she proud of herself? Does this person have any doubts? Does this person have to ask for approval or permission? Is she confident in herself? This is what I want understood and recognized without asking! This is the person! That can stand there and tell you just how she is feeling. This is the person! I have always wanted to be! This is the person! I hope to become. I guess what I'm saying is, can you see who this is? Can you accept who I am? I know this sounds like alot of crazy talk but it is real important to me. You would have to be in me to understand that. I want to express all that I am but when I do, I hear many different voices talking in my head as if everyone is talking at once and I try to the best of my ability to sort it out and then bring it out. I cannot believe I am trying to put this down on paper, and I am trying to make some kind of sense of it. When I try to put my feelings down on paper, I feel a rush of emotions. It is as if a wave comes over me. When this happens I will see this little girl and she will look so lost and scared. I'll see her look around as to say where am I? Or where is everybody? Then quickly I will think of something else, or see pictures of Ryan, or hear him talk to me. If you think this is confusing to you just think of how it is like for me. Sometimes or I should say almost all the time, I say to myself do not share these feelings, it does not make sense. If, I start to share I hear myself say; what is that? What you just said, do you think anyone wants to hear that or cares what that means? So what if that is the way you feel. Keep it to yourself. No one wants to hear all that crazy stuff. I fight with myself to talk and sometimes it takes allot of energy. With all this, I am still grieving for Ryan. Ryan is right there in the middle of all this trying to find a place. He is trying to find a place to fit and belong. I can hear him saying did you forget about me? I am still here and I am not going anywhere. The reason I feel so bad is because, he should be the only person I am thinking of. He is always there because I sense him and feel him but not in the way, you would expect me to. It is as if you know it in your head but cannot feel it because someone gave you a pill that numbed you. I do not like that feeling because I know it. I knew that, that is what was happening and I did not have any control over it. Who gave them the right to take away my feelings? I decided to write because I know that no one can stop my train of thought and I have to say exactly what I feel even if it does not make any sense. I have to get it out somehow. I told myself before I started to write this. I told myself to go ahead and write it down, all it is, is words on a piece of paper and words cannot hurt you. They are just words after all. In addition, it cannot hurt because just maybe someone can make some sense of all the talk. If not, that is al-right too. Therefore, what I have decided to do is to start writing down my feeling more often. No matter what they sound like they are still my feeling and a feeling is a feeling and it does not always have to make sense. At least that is what I have been told on many an occasion. Sometimes I feel like I am in a maze. Running to find out where I am! When I first start out it is not too bad because I am thinking to myself this is not too bad, I can do this. Therefore, I go along content in my thoughts and somewhat at peace with myself. Then on certain days, it becomes scary and dark and lonely. I guess my imagination takes over and depending how I feel that day is the way I will experience the maze. I know in myself that I am moving, I know this because I can feel the movement. However, I have lost my way. I know if I were able to rise about the maze I could see my way so clear through every little turn. But I don't have that advantage. I have to feel my way around like a blind man. One advantage the blind man has over me is he has been blind and being blind he has learned how to walk in his blindness. The dark isn't scary to him. He uses his other senses to help him find his way. I guess I will have to become like the blind man and learn how to use my other senses to help me through the maze. There are days when I'm in that maze when I can feel my heart racing and pounding so hard I think I will lose my breath. There are other days when I feel confident I will find my way out and I'm not scared at all. Those are the days I feel like I could climb a mountain and still have energy to go on. While all of this is happening to me remember my outside life is still going on. I have an inside life and an outside life. We all do I believe. At least that is the way it is for me. I think when my inside life is happening that is the time I want to be alone with no intrusions. I feel good when I am there. I become almost angry when people invade that place, and break the silence and the sacredness of that place. I can go in and out of there at will when I choose to do so. I want to be the one to make the choice. When I started to write my feelings, my true feelings down I noticed some things about myself that I didn't notice before. I feel some relief and not as frustrated as I was before I started to write. It seems that forming these thoughts that I thought couldn't be formed gives me a feeling of self. No matter how confusing it may sound to anyone else it gave me voice and I put it out there and it is not just a thought flying around in my head banging against the wall of my mind making me feel crazy. As I write this, even now I'm saying to myself who is this person who is writing? They make a lot of sense. It can't be me. She sounds so together and says it just right. I'm looking at her and I see myself as if I were a child looking up at her. I want to grab her hand she seems so nice and smart. She is someone I want to be like. I want to get to know her. When I am looking at her as that child, I can sense Ryan standing there with me almost as if he was I. The two children seem to be best friends and they are always whispering cute things into each other ears. Why does that little girl seem so important t me? She seems so trusting and wide-eyed. When I think of her or see her in my mind, she always looks so lost. She looks as if she is looking for someone. How did she get there? Does everyone have a child they can see or hear? When this starts happening in my writing I want to stop because I know how this must sound to others and my logical mind does not want to hear it. But everything inside of me wants to keep going. It feels so good to talk. Therefore, I am going to keep writing as if no one would ever see my writings so I can feel safe to say anything I want. If I could talk to her, I would ask her about herself. I would ask her if she needed to tell me something or say something to me. I can barely hear her little voice. She told me I was not crazy and that she sees me too. She says I'm very strong and she likes that about me, and plays with me a lot. She thinks

I have a great sense of humor and hears me laughing a lot. She says we are no different than the rest of the world we just listen more than they do. We pay attention to our feelings more than most. We see far beyond what most people would even dare to dream. She says the reason she looks so sad is that she misses Ryan a lot. Ryan helped her not be so lonely. She doesn't know whether he could see her, but she thinks he did or just enjoyed her through me. I would like to let her keep talking, she seems pretty smart for a kid don't you think? When I'm writing I get this great sense of freedom I could write forever. I feel joy right now as I write. What freedom. If I could go on saying whatever I feel without the fear of someone making something different out of it I think I could write a book. I have some great characters in mind. I feel like I'm exploring myself for the first time. I don't even need a map. I hope I can keep writing. I hope this wont stop. I don't want it to stop. It's pretty neat and it feels so good. I have to stop now I have to go to work. Talk to you later.

My Story

When I brought Ryan to the emergency room late one night in February, he was six and a half years old. Little did I know my life was about to change forever? I carried Ryan to the back of the emergency room. He felt like a wet dishcloth. He was lifeless. They took him out of my arms and started to call his name and shake him to see if he would respond. Ryan didn't respond so they called a code blue. I stood there almost breathless as I watched this scene unfold right in front of me. I felt like I was not there. It felt so surreal. I saw him having seizures one after another. He had at least three. He also had stroked-out which blew both his eyes. The doctors and nurses were trying everything they could to save his life. Here was my helpless child and lying there and I could do nothing to help him. I felt just as helpless watching this happening right in front of my eyes. We as parents are never prepared for a thing like this to happen. Ryan ended up in a coma that lasted for three days. They were three of the longest days of my life. I did not sleep or eat at all I was on automatic at this point.

When Ryan came out of the coma, we still did not know what had caused all the many things that happened to Ryan in the emergency room because of this they had to run a whole gamut of tests and that took days. Once again, I found myself waiting breathlessly for them to come back with an explanation of why these things happened, while praying all the time that it was nothing serious. I will never forget the day when the results came back. Here is where it gets hard to write but I am going to try. That day the doctors got together and brought us to the room at the end of the hallway. I will never forget that room. I can still see it and smell it, as if it was yesterday. This is the room where they bring parents. It was the place where you are told the best news or worst news of your life. In my case, it was the worst. The very worst a parent can ever hear. They told me that they had discovered a large

28

mass inside Ryan's gut region. As soon as I heard the word mass my ears no longer heard anything! I know I was there physically but mentally I was gone! Gone! Gone! I think apart of me is still gone. Along with that terrible word mass, came the last name in the world you would want connected to your child. It was the worst word, you could ever imagine. Nevertheless there it was bigger then life itself and living in my baby, my precious little boy Ryan. I don't think I could think for along time after. I just couldn't et it into my head. Ryan was in really bad shape. Ryan had lost a lot of weight and was very weak but he was very much the fighter, as many would soon find out. It was then, I knew we were in a fight and it was going to be a true fight for our lives, but in reality it was Ryan's fight because he would be the one who would have to go through all the things they were going to put him through. Ryan did go through all the operations and procedures and chemotherapy protocols. He went through them with very little, if any complaints. It is amazing when I think of it now. Here was this little six year old showing us how to do it. I will always admire Ryan for his courage and strength. Ryan you were and are the greatest kid a mom could want. I am going to share with you now, something I could never admit when Ryan was alive. As soon as I heard the news about Ryan having cancer, somewhere deep down inside me I knew I was going to lose my child. Nevertheless, even though you think that you always have hope and I had plenty of that for Ryan. He was the meaning of the word hope. His eyes said it.

His Laughter said it. How could you not have hope for your child? A child symbolizes hope.

So, can you see how when Ryan died part of me died too! I invested a lot of me in Ryan. We kept our mental energy at a high at all times. No matter what the doctors said because we believed that even if you got a bad report, if you kept positive attitude in your thinking it could change things. In the last few weeks of Ryan's life we took the word celebrates to a new level. Even people in my own family thought I was losing it. I know it could look that way to some but from where I was coming from I did not think so. I wanted Ryan to know that even if his eyes were staying closed, we as family and friends were not going to give up on him. No matter what, he was going to hear his family and friends living because he was still living and this was not a time for a funeral. Funerals are for dead people. He was not dead! He was very much alive! He was especially alive in the spirit. Ryan did more things in the last week of his life without saying a word. Just by who he was. I could go on forever about Ryan and the way he viewed life. So let me say this in closing. There is no way I could ever make anyone understand what losing Ryan is like for me. I can only say I am a changed person forever. I am forever changed in a good way. I will be forever sad about Ryan's death. And as I spend the rest of my time here on earth there will be a hole that nothing can fill because that hole belongs to Ryan. I will be forever missing his beautiful smile and more so his laughter. I will miss his beautiful eyes that told you everything. I will miss his eyes because they could not hide a thing. I will miss forever his voice that said; "hi mom, I love you!" I will forever miss his arms that gave me great hugs! I will forever carry a mother's sorrow and I will bare this in my heart until I meet him again in heaven.

My Words in Tears

Ryan! Ryan! Ryan! I miss you so much today I don't care where you are at I just want you. Oh God why did this happen to my sweet Ryan? Why? Today is one of those days I cannot see the bigger picture, all I can feel is the missing of my boy. Can I please have him back now please? Ryan I am so sorry I did not get to check it out before you went. To make sure you would be safe. Every mother wants to make sure it is safe where are children go. I am trusting God the best I can that it is a wonderful safe place without pain and tears. I sometimes feel guilty that I told you not to worry and not to be afraid of dying that when you die you go to heaven to be with God. I saw that trust in your eyes because you always trusted me without question. So now, I have to trust my feelings, about death and dying and myself and Heaven.

And if, I was to be totally honest here, and that is what I truly want to do. I want others to see that even the faithful can be faithless and question our own beliefs. This is part of the growing process. That God loves us just as much when we question, or when we go by faith. To say we do not understand is not to say we do not believe, or we do not trust. It is saying in truth, what is in our mind but do not dare to speak. To speak it is to say it is the truth of how you feel. This I think is why people who are in tough times do not talk or share their feelings because if they did they feel that they might be judged as not believing or being faithless, when nothing could be further from the truth.

I personally feel that God would be the first to understand and give his permission to feel however, we feel. I think that people put into Gods mouth words that he wouldn't even think to say. I think that people should be left alone to say how ever they feel that day maybe tomorrow they will not feel that way, or maybe they will, who knows? I think people should be allowed to feel the full range of emotions all of them have a purpose whether you agree or not. My hope for myself is to first give myself permission then experience the feeling honestly and openly and then somehow stay with the one that causes spiritual growth that will someday or maybe never afford me an answer to my question

Remembering Ryan

I often remember the times late at night when Ryan and I went to bed. He would like to sleep with me. That is when all the days' activities were over. With no more playing left to do Ryan would start his wonderful mind going to ask me the most amazing questions a little boy his age could think of?

One night he asks me a question. He asked me, "Mom why does God allow such evil in the world"? How would you like that for a question just before you were getting ready to go to sleep? Moreover, believe me you would have to answer Ryan when he asked a question. I would say I do not know Ryan, but someday we will have that answer. Another time I remember Ryan asking one of those kinds of questions, it was early evening and he was going to the bathroom. I know that sounds strange, but this was a common thing with us he would be in the bathroom and I would be on my bed were he could see me. Ryan did not like the bathroom door closed. He always wanted to see me. Therefore, he is sitting there spinning the tubes that were coming out of his chest. They were the tubes they used to give him chemotherapy and medications and blood and thinking as usual, and he asked me this question.

When they nailed Jesus to the cross, did they know whom they were killing? I thought about it for a minute and said yes they knew it was Jesus. Then Ryan said I know they knew it was Jesus but did they know he was God? Talk about being dumbfounded. Would you ever expect that from a 7 year old? Ryan would definitely keep you on your toes. My answer to him was if they did not know then, they sure do now. What else could you say to that? Ryan had this amazing way of making everyone feel loved. In order to show you the real Ryan, I have to share some family stuff I hope my sister will understand I think she will. There was this time on one of the very last times Ryan came home from the hospital. My sister has had a drinking problem for years and she would go off of the wagon on occasions. And this one-day she called and I could tell she had been drinking, so I started yelling at her on the phone and telling her not to come over the house if she had been drinking. I did not want to upset Ryan's visit home. I was still yelling at her when Ryan noticed whom I was talking to on the phone. He called out to me and said; hey mom is that my Aunt Cathy you are talking to on the phone. Tell her to come over. Tell her she can come any time she wants. So what if she has a social problem I still love her.

Months later he showed me just how smart he was because one day when I was laughing he saw right through me. He said hey mom why are you laughing? Do you have a laughing social problem or something? Everyone in the room laughed so hard, but not me, what he said cut me right to the quick. Ryan knew exactly what he was saying. He knew what I needed to hear, even if I wasn't ready to hear it. Ryan got me right where I lived. He knew how to get to my soul. I realized I am no different than my sister. We all have problems. Just some are more noticeable then others. I still cannot get over what a smart kid he was.

Remembering Ryan brings up so many different feelings. The first feeling that comes up is a tremendous feeling of sadness and total emptiness and isolation compounded by this sense of not realness. Moreover, in that not real place you are trying to make some sense of death and dying. In particular your son's death! Along with that come mixed feelings, of happiness and joy for living because Ryan did it so well. He loved playing practical jokes on everyone. He had a real zest for life not even cancer could quench. Ryan literally looked death in the eye and laughed. Right to the end we laughed and played to the best of our ability. Ryan's room was filled with life. His room was full of the music that was played to the dancing that was done by his cousin Samantha. You had a real sense of heightened life. When you are that close to death, if you let it, you can feel more of life. I know that makes no sense, but it's true just ask the people that came in to Ryan's room in those last few weeks they will tell you. Just ask the Doctor's, Nurse's, anyone willing to share what they felt. I think what really brings it home is the fact that it took a little boy with great courage to do it first. Almost like we should have been showing him, he was showing us. That's where that strange feeling comes in and won't let you go. I hope I can explain this. God please help me here.

I think the reason why all of us talk about this strange feeling that is to hard to put into words is just this. All of us just go about our lives going to and from work not thinking about life or the meaning of it. Then without warning something like this happens to us. A little boy we all love gets Cancer. That knocks us back for a while. We know it is there but just cannot believe the worst. So we go on thinking everything is going to be all right. There is no way you could think he would die but as time went on and the reality of the situation starts to show itself. So now you have to make a choice here. Do I stay? Or do I go? For those who choose to run, I would say they missed-out on the greatest experience of their life. For those that choose to stay they will have had the greatest experience of their spiritual lives. Now here comes the hard part for me. I now have to learn a new way to experience Ryan. This is not an easy task to say, never mind to do. To even say it, it will require allot of time. I still want to the flesh of Ryan! I do not want the spiritual Ryan yet, maybe in time I will, my arms still miss my little boy to hug.

My lips still miss the softness of his skin. I still miss kissing him goodnight. My ears still miss the sound of him calling me mommy. My nose still miss's the smell of his hair when I hold him at night, as he lies sleeping. So you see it will be a long time before I can accept the death of Ryan. How can a mother ever accept the death of her child! To say you accept the death of your child is to somehow say you agree. The word is definitely not to accept. I do not know what the word is yet and when I do, I will let you know

Ryan as a Man

I was sitting in the courtroom on the day that Ryan was sworn in as a policeman. I saw my little boy sitting in the front row he had no idea that on this day he was going to be sworn-in as a police officer. Until director Neapolitan called Ryan up and told Ryan, he was going to become a policeman this day. Ryan was beaming and he got the biggest smile on his face. It made me cry to see him so happy. There was my little boy busting with pride. When Ryan stood up, all at once, I looked at him and I did not see my little boy. I saw a very tall dark and handsome young man so ready to serve his Community. Ryan would have been a great policeman. He had all the right qualities. He was never judgmental. Being fair is what Ryan was about. He liked bringing people together in a peaceful way. He did that with us at home he never liked fights. He would always try to see the other person=s point of view. I know that sounds like a lot for a small boy but truly that is how Ryan was.

I remember one time in the hospital I was having a discussion with Danielle and Ryan chimed in with this. Mom, I suppose you never were nineteen before. I guess you don't remember. Leave her alone, and she will be ok Mom. Not only did I lose the best little boy, a mom could never want but the world lost out on the best man for the job. I often think of the man my Ryan would have been. I can see him now coming over to the house saying Hi Mom. How is the prettiest woman in the world doing today? Do you have something to eat? I will forever miss Ryan the man. What I really saw was the biggest man in my life and he was embodied in my eight-year-old son.

When Ryan died on that Sunday I will never forget, his partner Officer Joseph Walker came I asked him to please escort Ryan to the funeral home. I couldn't bear the thought of him being alone. Ryan was buried with full policemen's honors. Four cops carried his coffin.

He had an Honor guard and bagpipes at the gravesite. The most moving funeral I have ever seen. In addition, many who attended told that to me. They said I have never seen a little boy demand so much respect. He was that kind of kid. Many would say about Ryan. The boy who would be man, but I say the man who would be boy. For he will always be, my boy. He will be forever and ever my boy Ryan.

Ryan's Heart

I am sitting here trying to put down on a piece of paper the most painful feelings a mother could describe. How do you express in words on a piece of paper the loss of a child? Where do you begin? I guess I will start with Ryan. Just Ryan I guess!

Inside Ryan's heart, lie all my dreams and hopes and wishes for a lifetime. In Ryan's heart are all those sweet smells of youth and tender feeling.

Locked in his heart forever is the love of his family and friends. He has taken with him to heaven. So a little of us all is in heaven now with him.

I can see him now having conversations with the sage's of old. I remember not long before Ryan died I was standing by his bed just watching him sleep, you know just trying to drink up as much of him with my eyes as I could before he died.

I do not know how to explain this except to say he spoke to me with his mind. He said mom remember the time you had that dream or vision you shared about me before I was born? And I was looking over heavens wall searching and searching the world over until finally I said there, there she is. That is the one I want to call my mom.

Well mom you almost had it right. Now go to the other side of the bed. Go ahead. Go to the other side of the bed. I will tell you how it really was.

You see you mom. You and I had a conversation a very long time ago in a different time and place very far from here. You said to me how I could get to where you are at and I told you. I also told you it was not an easy thing to do. I told you that in fact, it would be very hard and mostly painful. It would be through a death experience. It would be through the death of a child. I said I would be the child if you would be my mom and serve me through my death. So you see mom you almost had it right. It was you that picked me, not me picking you. And yes I did come to help you but just not in the way you thought. It was for a spiritual reason.

That is why God has come out of the box for you and along with him coming out he took all of your scaffoldings. Mom, please do not be afraid of the God that came out. He is not

So big of a god, that you cannot have a personal relationship with him. He is the same yesterday, today and tomorrow.

Now this is the thing I want you to remember while you are here on the earth. Whenever you are going to make a decision or a judgment on a person always remember the other side of the bed. It is the same idea but a different perspective. Things always look so different from the other side of the Bed.

I want you to be kind and gentle when judging a fellow human. Most of all is kind and gentle to you. So, can you see why it would be so hard to let go of Ryan, who in their right mind would want to let go of the best kid in the world? I often thought about that and realized. When Ryan said those things to me that was no child talking to me I didn't know exactly what or who it was. I now believe that was a very old and wise soul. I think when children die young they are very old souls that don't need to spend a lifetime to share their understandings of life. They just come and share their message and leave. Ryan was an old soul; I just didn't know it at the time because for me he was my Ryan, just Ryan my sweet baby boy.

Ryan's Room

On Ryan's room so many different things happened and I hope during the course of my writing I will get as much of it down as possible.

On this one day, or I should say over a long time and many hospital stays when I had been answering everyone's questions. They asked the same questions repeatedly, I could see, for Ryan he was getting sick of answering the many questions. So Ryan said to me. Moms please make me a big sign and have the sign read as follows. Do not talk to me! I said sure Ryan and I made the sign for him. Of course being the mom, I made the sign with one word added and that word was PLEASE in capital letters. I told Ryan you have to put the word please in there. It is not nice to just say do not talk to me. Ryan did not argue the point he knew I was right. So the sign that would be so much a part of Ryan's room found it's way over Ryan's head on the monitor right below the scripture verses for Ryan' healing.

This sign was great for Ryan. I think it gave him a feeling of some kind of control over something, because he had no control over what was being done to him; and most importantly over the cancer that was growing quickly and stealing his young life right out from under him. Doctors would come in the room just to see how he was doing. They would ask a question and Ryan would point at the sign. Sometimes it would work and sometimes not. This would go on for weeks. It was funny to watch. I got a great sense of Ryan's character. Because, believe me he had a great sense of character. The many people would came into Ryan's room after the sign went up and as they did, so to did his hand point to his beloved sign that expressed his feelings so well without having to say a word.

Let me tell you this, there was no joke in this for Ryan. He meant it when his hand went up. He was saying clearly. What is everyone' problem can people read? Sometimes he would get so frustrated he would make sighing sounds and roll his eyes back. Until one day out of shear frustration, he said to me. Mom take the please out of the sign! With that, I replied why Ryan and he looked at me and said no one sees it anyhow. So I crossed out the please and the sign worked better. It seems people pay more attention when you say Do Not talk to me.

Ryan's Voice

Ryan's voice is like no other voice I know. It has a sweet sound and is very magical. Sometimes it can only be seen and yet not heard. Sometimes it can only be felt in the warmth of a sunny day, or a clear moonlit night. Sometimes the sounds are in your memory of the days when you shared a touch or a thought about the mysteries of the universe and pondered together the meaning of life. I often miss the sound of his voice where the child like sound reminded me of the purity, and innocence of his youth, and most of all his unquenchable thirst for knowledge.

What amazed me the most was the wisdom and compassion in the simplistic way he saw life. He never complicated life at all. He just lived each day like it was a gift.

I am now learning to find the voice of Ryan in a different way. I hear his voice in all the things he loved. He talks to me in the beauty of a sunny day. He talks to me in the stillness of the night. He sings to me in the summer breezes as they blow through the leaves. He speaks to me in my heart. He speaks to me when the pain is rushing over me like a title wave. And I hear him say mom I am all right. I am right here and I love you and miss you too!

Ryan's voice can still be heard in all the people who carry his memory. He is alive in the truest sense. His voice will be heard in the way they see life and view their children. If they have ears to hear, they will see the beauty and wisdom that stands right in front of them. If they allow themselves to see life like a child and welcome it with open arms and hearts, they too will hear the voice of Ryan, because that is where he lives. He lives in the purity of your child like way of looking at life.

He will always have voice as long as the child lives within you as long as you give it freedom to express its voice in all you do. Don't be afraid of the child because the child is you and you are the only one that can give it voice.

Saying Goodbye

Saying goodbye, I say it at least ten times a day. Saying goodbye is a part of our everyday life. I never thought much of it until my beautiful eight-year-old son Ryan died of a long battle with cancer that word would just roll off my tongue. When I was in the grocery store and saw a friend, or when I was on the phone my last words were always goodbye. I look at that word, and many other everyday words very differently now. Words hold a lot more meaning then they did before Ryan died. I hear the words differently, and nothing is simple or easy. Everything takes on new meaning.

I now live in a world where goodbye doesn't mean I will see you later, or until next time. It means goodbye to this moment in time. I have spent with you. Goodbye to a moment in time that was shared and will never happen again. It means goodbye to goodbye and hello to, I will see you again. People don't think much about the word goodbye; it is just a word you say to move on. Like in the grocery store or when you are on the phone. It is a closing of that moment in time. It is in essence, a period to mark the end of that brief moment and allows you to go on to the next.

Goodbye just helps us to mark the spot were one moment starts and where the next will begin. Good-byes allow us to mark that time and place in our minds so we can reflect and savor even the sounds and smells of that moment in time. Goodbye is just the springboard to help us move on and shouldn't be looked at as a final ending of that moment in time. It should be looked at as a different and new beginning of an old moment that will carry a lot of the old into the new.

So you see the simple word goodbye, will never be the same for me. I think a lot more about it now than I ever did before. Who said goodbye had to be good? How could it ever be good to say goodbye to your son? Or any love one? The good is not in the goodbye, it is in the way we choose to live with what has happened to use as survivors. It is what we do on this side of the goodbye. There are always two sides to a goodbye. There is ours, and there is their'. So from this side of my goodbye I would like to tell my son Ryan, goodbye to my wonderful little boy and my best friend and hello to the new me who would like to meet the new you, and never have to say GOODBYE again.

PS: Goodbye for now

Silent Pictures

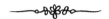

As I stand here and in my mind's eye I feel as if I am waiting for something, or someone. I feel like I am on a street corner looking down the road. Then all of a sudden it happens, pictures start to appear out of nowhere. They pass as if they are in a silent parade. They pass by like a parade with no music or marching bands. They are just pictures of moments, in a fragment of time, which brings with it, it is own sounds and images to be felt the very moment it appears in front of you. There are times during the parade that you feel like you are fighting the crowd to get a better view and you are pushing your way to the front in fear that you will miss something. Something that will never be seen again, that you can't just let it pass by. Once you get to the front and start to view the parade you realize you have to pick and choose the things you view because there is just so much stuff happening. There is just too many things to look at. What things do I save? What things do I choose to remember? Which ones will I cherish years down the line?

One thing I have noticed about the parade is it doesn't stop for anyone, and all those that see it, view it differently. Everyone remembers things that touched them and brought them to either laughter, or tears. These silent pictures and images have now formed a scrapbook in my mind that I can turn to visit the day I saw you in my parade of pictures passing silently before me, gently moving me to that time and place where I can breathe the sweet smells of yesterdays and hear you in the sounds of my tomorrows where, forever joins my beginning with your ending.

Tell Me This Is A Dream

ell me this is a dream! Please would someone tell me this is a dream! Would someone please wake me up from this nightmare? This has to be a dream! Because, it is too horrible to believe that it is real. How could it be real? To say it is real is to say you are gone. How could you be gone? My beautiful little boy with the most beautiful smile is not here to hug his mom and ask all those wonderful questions about life. Would someone please be kind enough to wake me from this nightmare! I cannot believe you are gone Ryan. I only had you for eight short years.

We just got started on this road together of discovering each other. I was just starting to learn how to listen to you as a real person who had his own way of seeing things. You were teaching me how to pause and stand back and observe before I said something. You taught me how to take it all in and to appreciate all that was happening around me before I said the first thing that was on my mind.

It was you! It was you my son, who was my teacher and I was your student and not the other way around. Your death has taught me so much about myself. Your death taught me things I would have never learned on my own. Your death has forced me to grow even when I did not want to.

I just wanted to stay in my own world of the pain over losing you. I wanted to stay in that world of my own making so I could hold on to you with that pain. But you being who you are would not have it that way. You would not allow me to stay there in that place of pain without moving on. You let me know it is okay to visit but I cannot stay. Living in that place was not going to honor that you were as a person, because you were a person who was full of life, and enjoyed being alive. You celebrated every moment you were here and wanted me to know you still are.

Many days I wanted to pretend this did not happen. I think about the days when you went to school on the bus, and I would worry if you got there all right, and if you were missing me the way I as missing you. When you first died I would pretend you went to camp and were going to be gone for a while, but you never came back. It was then I realized you were never coming back. No matter how much I cried and begged and pleaded with God, you were not coming back.

This is when the reality of what happened started to sink in. Oh, my God! It is really true. Ryan, you are not coming back! I wish this were a bad dream or nightmare. At least I would know that someday I would wake up and find you here with me.

I wish this were a dream, because it would mean I have more time with you. I would have more time to hold you and kiss you and smell your hair. I would have more time to look into those beautiful brown eyes that looked at the world with such wonderment. More time to tell you I love you and hear you say you love me too. More! More! more.! I just want more. So would someone please do me a favor? Please wake me up from this dream and I will forever be in your debt. Please say it is not so. Thank you.

The Big Little Man

◦⊶❦⊷◦

I sit back, and take a deep breath, and let it out softly. Then I close my eyes to once again see your beautiful face. Oh how I miss your face Oh to just touch it again. I would love to hold you and tell you how much I miss you my son. That a day doesn't go by without me wanting to give you a hug and kiss. I miss your kisses and great laugh and most of all your beautiful smiles that invited me to share a part of your soul.

You are my love forever. It is you who taught me the meaning of life. I will forever be in your debt. It was your dying that brought me to a self-realization. It was your death, which started me on this journey down a path of enlightenment. It is a path that was and still is a very painful one. It was this path that was paved with human tears and sorrow, and a path that was forged through some of the darkest moments a soul can ever imagine possible.

It was you my son, with the help of God who gave me the courage to go on each day. It was in your courage and strength that I found mine. It was in the way you lived your life, which I found my way back to mine. How could I not go on living when you lived your life to the fullest, even when you were dying at the time? You showed all those around you what the true gift of life is.

You showed all those around you how very important it was too appreciated every minute we have, because we never know when our lives could come to an end. You showed us all what it like to look death in the eye, and not only look it in the eye, but do it with grace and humility.

My son, there are no words that can express your mothers pain and sorrow over losing not only my sweet little boy, but my best friend and forever after ending me once imagined for you. I not only lost my sweet little boy. I also lost my future hopes, wishes and dreams of a lifetime filled with you. I lost a lifetime of memories waiting to be made. I lost the handsome man that would someday walk down the aisle with his beautiful bride in hand. I lost the beautiful grandchildren that would remind me of you when you were a little boy.

What I will have and keep forever is the memory of a brave little boy who on many occasions was every bit of a man you could ever want. He was in the body of my little boy. He was the man many would have wanted to be if they were in your shoes. The truth is they couldn't fit the shoes, and not because they were too small but because they were too big.

So you see my little man, what you left us when you died was a lot to think about. You left us to think about the way we live our lives and what we do with the life we have. You left us to figure out what is important and what is not. You left us to think about the purpose of your coming. It is up to us to search our souls for the answer if any. You were the source and reason for their journey and mine too. I will always think of you as my little boy, but in reality you are the biggest man I ever knew and I am blessed to have been your mother.

Love Mommy

The Road Goes Both Ways

⁓⊶⧬⊷⁓

This is not an ordinary grief book. What I mean by that is it is not one like most of the grief books you find on the bookshelves in a bookstore. It is really very ordinary because it is written by a very ordinary person like me. It is my personal journal with my feelings about how it feels for me to lose a son. A beautiful little boy named Ryan Michael. Ryan is actually the seed for my writings. He is first, the reason I write, and second, the cause for all my feelings and the need to express them. If I didn't write, I don't know how I would have made it this far. When I write my feelings down, I don't know it at the time, or didn't know it in the beginning, that it was part of the healing process. I know it now because I can see and look back at some of my first writings and see the difference in the way I felt on those days. I saw the anger and the loneliness, the despair and how life had no meaning anymore. I saw the isolation and emptiness of the days following Ryan death. I could feel the feeling of not wanting to go on. If it wasn't for my writings, I would have kept all that stuff inside and it would have made me bitter. It would have been like poison. It could and would have destroyed me.

I think when Ryan died he left me a gift. Of course I didn't see it at the time. I was too busy grieving the loss of him. I thank Ryan every day for the gift he left me because through his gift I hope to help others find theirs. I think we all have a book inside us ready to be born. Born through the pain of losing someone we love very much. I think we all have untapped feelings and need to express them and share them with others. Too either validate those who are going through the same thing, or express to others what this is like, which will better help them to understand what we as parents are going through.

The road to the other side goes both ways. Sometimes we feel like the road only goes one way. This road is not l, where you have two ways to travel. It is up to us to choose which side we want to travel. I must admit there are times I find myself on the other side and that is okay too. Sometimes we need to travel backwards to regroup and plot our course. Backwards isn't always a bad thing. Sometimes there may be things we missed the first time around. So don't be afraid of going backwards, going backwards just affords you the opportunity to correct and to make smooth the road ahead. This road is a well-traveled road, but most of the time we find we are the only ones on it. We don't realize that because we are the only ones on it doesn't mean no one else has been there before us. If we stay on the road long, enough eventually you will meet other travelers and share with them your stories. Sometimes you may even cry together or better yet and on an occasion laugh together. The road is not always a sad road. Yes, for the most part it is sad, but believe it or not you can find joy and happiness on the road that goes both ways you just have to look for it, and search it out. Nothing comes easy on this road. You have to work hard at finding peace and contentment. Nothing's a given, not even in grief.

I should say especially in grief. You have to work twice as hard. The road that goes both ways is not a road that anyone chooses to go down. It is a road that we as parents are forced down like a detour we meet in the road. Forcing us to go places we didn't plan. But somehow, like the detour, it will bring us back to the road more familiar then the road where the rest of the world is on and to the road back into reality and to the road with directions to our next destination, to the road back to life.

The War of Grieving

———◦❦◦———

Grieving is like being at war with you. You are battling your mind for every piece of sanity you can get a grip on. The hardest part about this kind of war is that, while this war is going on you are still trying to live your life. I wish I could wear army fatigues because at least then people would know I was fighting for something, or I was in a battle of some kind. No one except close friends and family even knows you are in a war, even worst then that you are in a battle for your life and your sanity. In this war every day is spent looking out for land mines that could blow up in your face at any time. Can you imagine being in this kind of war? Now add to that, it is going to be a war that will never end. It will just change in the way you choose to fight it. If you are lucky maybe, you might have a truce once in a while. A time you can use to rest up for the next battle. It will be a time to tend to your wounds or time to gather your thoughts, so you can make your next battle plan.

If I was in a real war, I would look forward for the time I could once again be with family and friends to celebrate the victory over my enemy. In this kind of war who is my enemy and what is my enemy? Actually I have more then one. As I see it, I have three major enemies. They being death, time and life, death being death is my worst enemy. Death is my worst enemy because, death is the one you cannot beat and death does the most damage to you, because when death comes, he not only takes your life, he also takes your reason for living and your purpose. He is your ultimate enemy.

Time is another one of your enemies. He never stands still when you want him to. Time either, comes to fast or he comes to slow. Whatever the case may be, it is never what you want or when you want. Then there is life and you know life is always waiting for you. Life awaits you around every corner. And life also has its way of sneaking up on you when you least expect him and when he does, without notice he pounces on you with no mercy.

When you get a break from these three enemies, watch out for the little ones. The more subtle ones like memories, and feelings. They may not kill you but they can kick some butt when you least expect them to. So you see I am in a war. This war is the worst kind of war! It is a war I battle by myself. I have no comrades, no fellow soldiers.

Well maybe just some soldiers who are brave enough to enlist in a war that is not their own war and who will stay next to me for support, a few soldiers that are willing to put themselves on the line for me. It is a lonely war with no end in sight. It is a war that knows no boundaries. It is a war where everything is unfair and where, whatever is its motto. It's a war with no holds barred. It is an invisible war yet it is felt. It is felt by everyone who is close to you. In this army you are a soldier for life. I hope that someday in this war the battles will be fewer and I will not always be on the front line. And if I am really lucky and live through the war long enough I will see a truce and to know once again the meaning of the word peacetime. And I will find that real place of peace, where I can once again find true rest and a place where I can take a deep breath and find some relief from this terrible pain and keeping in mind there will always be a new battle down the road but my experience as a soldier will help me end the battles sooner and with less damage so I can get home faster.

The World Is Standing Still

The world stopped spinning the day I walked into Ryan's room and held his little hand as he was taking his last breaths on this side of heaven. I put his small hand in mine only to remember him saying "mommy hold my hand like this, this way you we always know it is me. Okay" and I said okay, Ryan just like this. Now as I was holding his hand for the last time I found myself staring at it as if I never saw his hand before. All I could see was my brave little boy taking his last breaths. I cannot even begin to tell you what I was feeling. How could you think when your mind is starting to numb itself because there could be no other way you could stand there and watch? If you really had an understanding for what was happening there could be no way you could stand there. Imagine watching your child die without doing a thing. I cannot to this day believe I just stood there and watched. I watched as they pronounced the time of his death. I felt like I was in a movie or a bad dream. As I stood there, I felt my mind drift to many memories of Ryan. One of my memories of Ryan that came to me was the very first time he walked on his own. I can still see the look on his face it was priceless!

He was beaming and smiling from ear to ear. What a big boy he felt like. As I stared at his hand, I could feel the warmth going out of it. Could this really be happening to me? God I hope not! But it was. God it truly was! Please God help me was all I could say in my head. Then another memory would come in. Flooding my mind to take the edge off what was really happening right in front of me. There was my boy dead in the bed. How could I let this happen kept coming up in my mind? Even though I knew in my heart I could not have stopped it no matter what? But all moms want to protect their babies from harm's way even if it is cancer that stands in front of her.

Ryan my brave little soldier fought a great battle against his enemy cancer with great courage and strength. He showed compassion for others during his long battle. Which brings to mind one of the many events where Ryan showed compassion for his fellow human. Once, on one of his last visits home I had to go to the store, so I asked my nephew Jimmy if he would not mind watching Ryan and his best friend Gilbert and his cousin Sam in the Park while I went to the store. When I left Ryan was swinging on a swing and smiling that beautiful smile of his. It made me feel so good to see him having fun. When I came back he was no longer on the swing like the other kids. He was sitting alone on a bench looking sad so I went up to him to see what was the matter.Ryan? I said Ryan why are you sitting here and not swinging like the other kids? All he could do was point. He was pointing at a man. So I said what about the man Ryan. I thought he was going to cry. He said Mom I am worried about that man over there, he just fell off his bike I think he has been drinking. Does he have anyone who cares about him? Imagine that coming from a seven year old. Little did I know how deep Ryan's feeling ran when it came to people? Ryan was all about people.

As I looked at Ryan lying there and pieces of the last 18 months would come flooding my mind. I remembered how we had to learn how to live with each other.

We had to learn when to back away and give some time and space to each other. Ryan and I did a lot of growing up together.

We had fights and cried together on many occasions. Sometimes, I was torn between trying to mother Ryan or just be his friend. I knew there was a great possibility that Ryan might never grow up so I would often allow him to become the man for a moment.

That, was the right he earned when he was diagnosed with cancer. Cancer was the robber of his youth. Each person deals with their situation differently. I chose to let Ryan voice his feelings anyway he wanted to even if I let him act like a grown up to do it. Believe me he fit the shoes most of the time.

He knew exactly what he wanted. He knew everything about his medications to the point that any new nurse would ask him and he would be more then willing to explain. What he got first and then next etc., etc. He learned how to manage his own pain. What an amazing kid, he was when it came to his own care!

Ryan's nurses had the greatest respect for him. They treated him like a man not a boy. Ryan demanded that and got it with no questions.

They knew what was happening to this little boy. How unfair it was. They allowed the little boy to become a man. Soon it was like it was normal. They just didn't see the little boy anymore. No one did. I don't know how it happened it just did. Everyone referred to Ryan as the old man. Something was happening right in front of us. We could sense it. You know you just give someone that look as if to say what is that? You just know when something unusual is happening? I would compare it to the feeling you get when you look at a rainbow. That good feeling you get way down deep in your soul. Ryan was that feeling.

The World Is Standing Still

The world stopped spinning the day I walked into Ryan's room and held his little hand as he was taking his last breaths on this side of heaven. I put his small hand in mine only to remember him saying "mommy hold my hand like this, this way you we always know it is me. Okay" and I said okay, Ryan just like this. Now as I was holding his hand for the last time I found myself staring at it as if I never saw his hand before. All I could see was my brave little boy taking his last breaths. I cannot even begin to tell you what I was feeling. How could you think when your mind is starting to numb itself because there could be no other way you could stand there and watch? If you really had an understanding for what was happening there could be no way you could stand there. Imagine watching your child die without doing a thing. I cannot to this day believe I just stood there and watched. I watched as they pronounced the time of his death. I felt like I was in a movie or a bad dream. As I stood there, I felt my mind drift to many memories of Ryan. One of my memories of Ryan that came to me was the very first time he walked on his own. I can still see the look on his face it was priceless!

He was beaming and smiling from ear to ear. What a big boy he felt like. As I stared at his hand, I could feel the warmth going out of it. Could this really be happening to me? God I hope not! But it was. God it truly was! Please God help me was all I could say in my head. Then another memory would come in. Flooding my mind to take the edge off what was really happening right in front of me. There was my boy dead in the bed. How could I let this happen kept coming up in my mind? Even though I knew in my heart I could not have stopped it no matter what? But all moms want to protect their babies from harm's way even if it is cancer that stands in front of her.

Ryan my brave little soldier fought a great battle against his enemy cancer with great courage and strength. He showed compassion for others during his long battle.Which brings to mind one of the many events where Ryan showed compassion for his fellow human. Once, on one of his last visits home I had to go to the store, so I asked my nephew Jimmy if he would not mind watching Ryan and his best friend Gilbert and his cousin Sam in the Park while I went to the store. When I left Ryan was swinging on a swing and smiling that beautiful smile of his. It made me feel so good to see him having fun. When I came back he was no longer on the swing like the other kids. He was sitting alone on a bench looking sad so I went up to him to see what was the matter.Ryan? I said Ryan why are you sitting here and not swinging like the other kids? All he could do was point. He was pointing at a man. So I said what about the man Ryan. I thought he was going to cry. He said Mom I am worried about that man over there, he just fell off his bike I think he has been drinking. Does he have anyone who cares about him? Imagine that coming from a seven year old. Little did I know how deep Ryan's feeling ran when it came to people? Ryan was all about people.

As I looked at Ryan lying there and pieces of the last 18 months would come flooding my mind. I remembered how we had to learn how to live with each other.

We had to learn when to back away and give some time and space to each other. Ryan and I did a lot of growing up together.

We had fights and cried together on many occasions. Sometimes, I was torn between trying to mother Ryan or just be his friend. I knew there was a great possibility that Ryan might never grow up so I would often allow him to become the man for a moment.

That, was the right he earned when he was diagnosed with cancer. Cancer was the robber of his youth. Each person deals with their situation differently. I chose to let Ryan voice his feelings anyway he wanted to even if I let him act like a grown up to do it. Believe me he fit the shoes most of the time.

He knew exactly what he wanted. He knew everything about his medications to the point that any new nurse would ask him and he would be more then willing to explain. What he got first and then next etc, etc. He learned how to manage his own pain. What an amazing kid, he was when it came to his own care!

Ryan's nurses had the greatest respect for him. They treated him like a man not a boy. Ryan demanded that and got it with no questions.

They knew what was happening to this little boy. How unfair it was. They allowed the little boy to become a man. Soon it was like it was normal. They just didn't see the little boy anymore. No one did. I don't know how it happened it just did. Everyone referred to Ryan as the old man. Something was happening right in front of us. We could sense it. You know you just give someone that look as if to say what is that? You just know when something unusual is happening? I would compare it to the feeling you get when you look at a rainbow. That good feeling you get way down deep in your soul. Ryan was that feeling.

Two worlds

The key to moving on after losing your child to death is all about learning how to live in two worlds at the same time. This takes time and a lot of practice and patience. The part that is so hard is to find balance between the two worlds. You have to be careful not to spend too much time in one world or the other. I am just learning how to find balance in both these worlds. I am not sure when it happened, it just did. I can tell you this though; it did not happen over night. It was through a lot of hard work and what I mean when I say that is just this. It is hard grief work. Believe me grief work is hard stuff and very tiring and mentally exhausting. I can tell you that first hand. The most important thing you have to do in grief work is be true to the experience. You have to honor where you are at, at all times. And what I mean by that is simply this. If you are having a bad day, just know that is what it is. A bad day that is all. Sometimes it is just what it is. You must be true to your feelings and express them. You cannot at this time, worry about the rest of the world, just be right where you are. You will only stay there as long as you need to. Remember this is your experience and no one else' after all this is your child we are talking about. No one had the relationship you did with your child. If I do anything with my book, the biggest point I want to get across is how the rest of the world has to back off and let us alone, (the grieving parent) when it come to grieving our children. If they could for one second see themselves in our shoes, they might understand how it feels to move on in a world that has no room for our children. Our children live in the other world we have made for them. A secret world filled with them. In this place we hold on to their laughter and see their tears. We hear them calling us mommy and can almost smell them. It is a sacred place. It is where shrines are made and reality has no ground to stand. Who wants reality in this place? We already have it in the other world we are forced to live in.

The world that has no more tomorrows for our children and that is enough reality for me. I can see how some of us never get to this place. It is so easy not to want to move or go on, as the world would put it. There are days when I feel myself back stepping and I know when I am doing it. The difference for me now is, I tell myself it is all right and I stay there as long as I want to. I do not allow anyone to pressure me out of there. I will come out when I am ready and when I do I am usually in a better place because I did just that. These are things you can only learn from the process of grief and time. This is what causes the healing to begin. It has to come from you and not from people's good intentions of trying to help you move on. It does not do you or them any good unless it comes from you alone. I often think how I wish I could have learned all this stuff without having to pay such a high price, or I should say Ryan having to pay the price. I know I am a different person now. I do not think like I use to at all. Ryan's death took with it many things. It took the old me and replaced it with this person I am trying so hard to get to know. I am learning about her every day. I think I could really get to like her if I would just let her in and find a place, a place she can call home. A very special place where Ryan lives on and he will never leave. It is just a matter of me understanding the bigger picture. I know someday I will, but for today, I just want to stay here a little longer. It is not my time yet.

Understanding

-------◦❀◦-------

*I*t is a few days before Christmas and the pain is so bad. I still cannot believe you are gone. Everything inside me screams to hold you. I cannot stand the thought of where you are. I know you are not in the ground but it still bothers me to think of your body being there. I want to hold that body so much. I find myself sitting here and pulling out my hair just from the thought of it. It is during these times that I feel left out of the rest of the world. Everyone is so busy getting ready for the day I do not want to come and the day where you will not be there to wake up and open up your presents like all the rest of the kids. The day I would love to sleep through. The day no mother who has lost a child wants to see come without their child in it. What I miss is the list you would give me with little stars next to the most important things you wanted. The one's most hoped for. I miss filling you're stocking and putting out cookies and milk for Santa. I miss when you would wake up and say Mom, look Santa ate the cookies and drank some of the milk and I would have to hold back the laughter because I ate the cookies and drank some of the milk, even if the milk was a little warm.

You were my invitation to visit Christmas through your eyes. Christmas will never be the same for me. I don't know how I will ever feel good at Christmas again.

I don't know how I will ever feel good again about anything. You allowed the child in me to come out and play with you and now that child is very lonely for you. She doesn't know how to come out. She doesn't want to come out without you. I can't even begin to describe what this feels like. God it is so bad.

Talking about God, which is another thing I am having a hard time with. My relationship with God has changed a great deal. I am right now in the building process, putting it together one piece at a time. I have to admit I lost my way when Ryan first died. I don't share that with too many people because they always have a pat answer like God knows best, or he has the whole picture. I know they mean well but that just makes it worse for me. I want to say to them would you say the same thing if you lost a child? Think about it would you? I don't think so. I know I love God, but just like if you were mad at your mother or father and they did something you did not agree with it does not mean you do not love them; it just means you do not understand them. You do not have the understanding or maturity to accept their decisions on a given matter.

That is how I feel most days, and on the others I grapple with myself to try and understand something that there is no way you could understand. To reach out to God and say, help me God, please help me. I want to understand but when that pain comes all I can feel is lost. I feel lost like I was in the middle of the ocean without a life preserver, looking for something or someone to hold on to. I know this is going to be a long haul for me trying to get back into a world without my son Ryan. I know it will take everything inside me to push myself every day to go on. It will be the hardest job I have ever had. It will bring me to places I never thought possible. It will bring me to the very highest. And it will bring me to the very lowest. I will find out more things about myself then I ever dreamed possible. I will find some things about myself that I did not know before. I only hope through all of this I can find some piece of mind, some understanding of who I am and get a better understanding of who God is in all of this. I know he gives me permission to feel this way. That is why I love him. He understands.

Whispers from Heaven

ey Mom. Can you hear me? It is me Mom! Ryan. I have been trying to talk to you for a long time. I just want you to know I have never left you. I am right here by your side. I would never leave you, just like when I was with you on earth. I love you so much Mom and miss you too. I miss the days when we would talk about everything. Remember when I would play jokes on you, well I still do. I laugh just like I laughed when I was with you in body. If you listen, you can hear me if you want to. I laugh a lot here. I watch over you day and night, even when you are sleeping. I love to watch you sleep; because you look so peaceful.

Mom, it is so beautiful here. Heaven is complete peace. No loud sounds like there are on earth. The sound of heaven is like a beautiful humming sound that surrounds your very being. The light is like the warmth of the sun without seeing it in the air. The colors are pastel and soft to the eye. I am with Grandpa and Ruthie and Uncle Louie and Aunt Grace and a lot of people you do not know. You recognize everyone the instant you pass over. Mom, I want you to know I was with you when I passed. I wanted so much for you to see me standing right next to you. I had my hand on your shoulder and I was saying I'm okay mom. I'm ok. I really didn't want to leave you. I felt so bad to see you cry. You know I never liked to see you cry. I want you to know I am so glad to be out of that body; It was so heavy. That is the first thing I noticed when I left it. I'm lighter then air now.

I am still your little boy so don't worry if I changed. Yes, I have changed. I have changed in the way that I now have full understanding and I do not think as a child, but I will always communicate to you as your son, because this is how you will know it is me. You will always hear me the way you remember me. I am grown up in the spirit. I returned to the spirit I was before I came. I am proud of you Mom. I know this is very hard for you. My dying was for a reason and I knew going in I was to die so don't feel guilty. I came to open people's eyes, to make them think. Some people will get stuck in the fact that I was a child and won't be able to get past that. I hope they look beyond that and see the true reason. It was to make them stop and take notice of themselves and where they are at. I came to jolt them to awareness of others and to get past themselves. Try not to think too much about the physical part of dying you can get stuck there if you let yourself. Think more about the spiritual side of dying. That is where your life truly begins.

Words

Words! Words! Words! Where are you when I need you? Other times you seem to flow so easy. Where are you when I need to explain this very deep pain inside? Why do you fail me when I need you the most? You leave me with terrible words that sound so mean and nasty, and full of sadness, and anger. Lots of anger I have anger for losing a wonderful little boy who did not deserve to die and to die in such a terrible way.

All I can think about is yelling my brains out and punching out walls, and screaming, and screaming, and screaming. However, that will not do me any good because all the screaming, in the world will not bring Ryan back. Damn it, Damn it, Damn it. Words! Words! Words! What damn good are you? No good. There has to be another way to describe! this PAIN. What other words are there. I am in this place deep inside myself where no one can come and no one wants to come I am sure. No visitors here. Who would want to come visit me there? I have no friends here just all this pain and me.

I wish I could give voice to the pain. Moreover, if I did make a sound, what would that sound, sound like? I am scared of the sound it would make. It would make deep animal sounds! It would make wailing sounds like a wounded animal that was mortally wounded and about to die! I can hear the sound in my head and it sounds so sad. It sounds too sad too listen to. That place inside of me I am very much afraid of it. I am afraid of it because I am afraid I will not come back from that place and I am more afraid that maybe I will not want to come back.

Expressions Section B

A Blossom Found in a Broken Soul

*eep down I go to the vastness of my soul, spiraling down to escape the terrible pain. I go there to hide myself in a corner to curl up in a ball never to come out again. I go there to find the tranquil solitude of my oneness with you. It is in this place I will find my recovery my peace of mind. It is in this place I will bring with me, my brokenness and it will be accepted. It is in this place I will be soothed and comforted. I will hear your voice and I will know I am not alone. You will speak to me your truths and grow me, like a blossom on a vine that appears on a wall with no explanation of its beginning, just evidence of its beauty in an unseemly place.

It is to cause me to think and ponder the reality of such a miracle. It is to say to me without words that beauty can found in all places, especially broken places. Broken places make good soil for the seeds of growth, and understanding which brings with it a new vine and a new flower, a new blossom, a new Life.

Balance

———❦———

*Y*ou know, you are growing up spiritually, when you do not make a judgment on where you are at or feel guilty for not being where you think you should be. You also know this when you do not view god as a punishing god. Not having those feelings is the truest sign of growth. The way I can tell this is when I hear or read a spiritual truth it feels like I either heard it before or it just rings so true and feels right at home with me. I love being in this place with God. It feels so good not to put pressure on myself. I can just be me at all times. When I read a spiritual truth for the first time it either does one of two things. It either makes me cry or it makes me laugh. Either one it is conformation to my soul that I am at home here. When this happens to me, I could almost swear I have read this material before. It is a feeling you just shake your head at.

And when the world starts closing in and all the problems of life start to apply pressure to me, I just step back and think of a spiritual truth I have just read and it brings things into prospective for me. My problems start to shrink right before my eyes. In view of the bigger picture my problems fade to almost out of sight. It is hard to see your problem as big, when you look at it from this place.

To get to this place in God, you have to let go of self and what I mean by that is, you have to let go of the ego part of self. That part of yourself that thinks only of preservation. This is not the good self-thinking at all. It is the kind of thinking that actually stunts your growth and keeps you in a very small place with God. The best way I found to keep growing in God is this: When I see or sense I am focusing on myself about a situation. I realize I have a choice here. We always have a choice about where we go in our thinking. As soon as, I take the focus off me and put it out there in the bigger picture. The choice becomes easy. In order for this to work it has to be the first thought you have right after the negative thought comes in. You can't give yourself anything to crab onto, because it will, it also has a need to survive. It wants to persevere its self too.

Now it is at this point where you either get it or you don't. It is such a thin line between hearing the sense of it and just dismissing it as crazy thinking. I know I go through that all the time when I am coming into a new understanding or truth about God. The way I keep it straight in my mind is. I say to myself, don't complicate matters just keep reading or listening until you find the truth in it. Don't be afraid to go on. It can't hurt you to read or listen and it doesn't cost anything except a little time. And it will be time well invested in your search for self wouldn't you say? We invest ourselves in the dumbest things, why not something that could have an effect on your life forever.

I am just finishing my first book, I have written. It is through this book that the doors to my spirit and soul were open. It was a very painful to write because I share with you the depths of my pain over the death of my son Ryan to cancer. Although it was very painful to write it served as the greatest catalyst for my spiritual growth, if I would allow it to be. I had to make a choice early on in the book. I have to admit I couldn't rise to the occasion everyday. Sometimes I just had to honor where I was at on any given day. Sometimes that place was not a higher place. In fact it was a very low place, a place filled with my flesh and humaneness. It just wanted what it wanted period.

The more I come to know about God, the more I realize I know nothing at all. Now this could be a scary revolution if you let it. The more I learn the less I know. So what am I doing learning more, or learning less? Now you know you have come somewhere when you think like that. but where? There it is again, that thin line between sanity and crazy thinking. I am starting to wonder if I have gone off the edge. Part of me feels the best I ever felt in my place with God and the other part is saying: what the hell are you thinking about.

Being at home with myself

———◦•❀•◦———

As I process through my life now, what I am discovering is, even though I am comfortable as I can be with this new person who emerge out of the deviation of Ryan's death. I think what makes me feel broken or not whole is when someone shines a light on my broken-ness or weakness. I don't think anyone would like to have someone hold a mirror up to him or her at all times. My biggest struggle is just keeping my sanity every day that is a hard enough job without worrying about how, you are saying something or if you over stated something or not. I am not even giving much thought to that. I know deep down inside, I am different and I have accepted that.

It may seem to some that I need to fix something and that very well may be true. What I would say to that is this: what if, what you thought, I need to change or fix was just not noticed, or over looked, wouldn't that achieve the same goal and everyone would be happy.

This is really a hard thing to convey to people. The most important thing for me is very simple and one of the hardest thing to get people to understand. I just want something very simple. I just want to have people except me for who I am and by doing this, even through they have noticed my weakness, they are saying to me, you are okay. I wouldn't even know I had a weakness or a vault if they weren't pointed out and when they are pointed out it is only then, that I even notice them. This is the only time I truly feel different.

Dear Clueless

would like to share with you my pain but that isn't possible unless you have lost a child yourself and that I wouldn't want you to have to experience. So with that being said, I would like to say this. I will try to my best to understand you if you try to understand me. I lost my child. My life will never be the same. I will never be the same again. I will be different from now on. I no longer have the same feelings about anything. Everything in my life has changed from the moment my child left to go to heaven. I will, on some days be very sad and nothing you say will changes that so don't feel like it is your job to make me feel better on those days, just allow me to be where I am.

When you lose a child you not only lose your reason for living, you lose the motivation to go on. You also lose your sense of self. It takes a long time to come to some kind of understanding for why this has happened, if ever. Of course we who have lost children know we have to go on but we don't want to hear someone else tell us too. Especially from someone who has not lost a child. It makes me and anyone who has lost a child want to say who are you to tell me that? Did you bury your child? I don't want this to sound like I don't appreciate everything you say because I know you mean well, but I just want you to appreciate where I am coming from too. I want you to understand that some of the things you say hurt me and others like me without you really knowing it. I know it must be pretty hard to talk to people like myself, not knowing what to say. That is why I am writing this letter.

If you don't know what to say, say nothing or just say I'm sorry. That always works for me. If you want to talk ad say my child's name feel free I would love to hear his name anytime. You not saying his name didn't make me forget it, or what happened to him. So by all means say his name. When special dates come or holidays come please forgive me if I'm not myself. I just can't keep it up on those days. I may wish to be by myself so I can think about my child without putting on a front. Most of all I want you to know I'm having a hard time with the death of my child and I am trying my very best to get back into life again. Some days it may look like I have accomplished that, and other days like I am at square one. And this will happen the rest of my life periodically. There are just no words to explain the living hell this feels like. There are no words that could ever do it justice. So please bear with me and give me time and don't put your own timetable on my grief and let me be the person I am now and not have to live up to the person you think I should be. Allow me my space and time and accept me for me. I will try my best to understand you.

Love Your Friend in Grief

Denial

enial is the best friend a person could ever want. It is always there to comfort them when the days get to tough. Other people would see it as something negative. It is a word full of despair or unreality. If you have not come to know Denial in that very personal way you would want to run from it as fast as possible. How could you want to be a friend to something that says: This isn't true, this is a dream you made up. You can make this what ever you wish it to be. On the other hand, why would you want to be a friend to something that will take away your life, as you know it? A life filled with unrelenting pain and sorrow and fills it with hope? I would say it sounds good to me. Does it not to you? What person in their right mind would not want a friend like that? Denial has been a friend of mine for a long time now. Longer then I realized. He has been there through thick and thin keeping up a strong front. The front was up against some distant cousins of his. They being distant have been trying to get hold of me for a long time and Denial, being there first, wanted nothing to do with them so he kept them away. I thank Denial for that because I'm not ready for their visit yet. No one seems to like my friend Denial. Why? He did not do anything to them. Why do they think he is such bad company for me? When Denial comes to visit he makes me feel good. He does not try to tell me things I do not want to hear. He respects me, and most of all he respects my feelings. He does not make me feel crazy. If anything I feel saner when he is around. Lately, Denial and I have been having some serious talks about him leaving. I don't want him to go. He says he has to. I asked him why and he said it was not good to over stay his visit. He said good friends didn't have to see each other everyday to stay good friends. He said good friends also know when it is time to leave. They are there when you need them the most. To comfort you through whatever problem you are having. He told me not to worry he would keep in touch and be there whenever I needed him. He said he was going to send me a couple of good friends of his to visit and for me not to be afraid of them. I told him I did not want any new friends. He was the only friend I needed and wanted. So Denial being who he was, wanted to stay too, but we kept on talking and he finally decided it was time to go. Not long after Denial left a good friend of his came to visit. His name was Anger. Anger came in and made himself right at home. He was very pushy and bossy. I did not like that at first. I found myself saying who is this person? I couldn't believe Anger was a friend of Denial. He was nothing like him. At first I did not like him because I could not understand him. There was not anything about him I liked. But as I got to know him and understand him we started to become friends. What I noticed most about my family and friends when Anger came to visit was they did not want to come see me much. they said when your friend Anger leaves we will come visit you. That put me in a bad position with my friend Anger and I know if I told him to leave he would be hurt. So what was I to do? I came up with a great idea. I told Anger if he would not mind hiding or to leave when my family and friends came to visit and he said sure as long as he didn't have to leave all together. So like Denial, Anger and me became good friends. Anger stayed with me for a long time and he too had a talk with me about having to leave and once again I found myself being abandoned by a good friend. Anger also told me he was not leaving me forever and he too would be there for me when I needed him. A long time after my two good friends Denial and Anger left, I found myself in a place that was so lonely words cannot even begin to express the desolation and emptiness of that place. There are people all around you yet you are totally alone in a crowd. I was really missing my friends. One day while standing in that place with all the noise from the crowd, I heard this faint voice. It seemed to be familiar. It called my name. I tuned it out for a long time. Then one day I found myself alone and not in the crowd. No sounds to distract me. It was then a person came up to me and said hello; do I know you? And I said I do not think so, who are you? He said first before I tell you, let me tell you this. I know a couple of good friends of yours and they told me to come see you. They told me to be very careful how I approached you. They also told me that you were very weary of strangers and to take my time when I introduced myself to you. So knowing that I waited and picked a time I thought was right. It was then I went up to you and said: I would like to introduce myself to you my name is Acceptance. As soon as I told you my name, you got up and ran. You ran so fast around every corner to lose me, this person called Acceptance. No way did you want any part of me. I do not know to this day, why you ran away so fast. I think there was something about my name. Acceptance. I am not sure to this day, what it was about my name. When I look back now and see you I question why you ran. Looking at myself from afar I do not seem so scary or mean or ugly. I think you just needed some time to check me out from afar. To approach me when you were ready. You needed to take slow little steps. You wanted to make sure you got to know more about me before you made me a friend. All your family and friends speak so highly of me. They say I come with great recommendations. It is funny how they did not want anything to do with your other two friends Denial and Anger and yet they like Acceptance! They must see something about me you did not. I know they only want the best for you. So I will take this under great consideration and thought the next time I come to visit you. Maybe, just maybe you will at least listen to what I have to say.

Expressions of grief

In this part of the book is where I share my personal feelings and my many different expressions of my spiritual process. This was my way of expressing the many different feelings that were born out of the pain of my grief. Some who are grieving may not be ready for this part of the book or maybe you will never want to be.

Your grief is your grief and I totally understand that. But if you want to continue please realize this is how it was for me and the way I choose to survive Ryan's death. I just kept writing and writing and writing and soon my writings started to change. I did not realize it at the time. But of course they would have too, after all I was changing everyday and I did recognize or even know it at the time.

I will share with you this: The grieving process is all about choices. I know none of us had a choice in the fact that we are grieving our children. But we do have a choice in how we will do that grieving.

In the beginning of the grieving process you just feel the pain. It is that pain that is hard to let go of. The reason we do not want to let go is because that sends a messages to us, the grieving parent. Letting go and the very message it sends is this: letting go somehow equates with, not only did we let go of the pain, but somehow it also sends the grieving parent the unwelcome message that we have somehow also let go of our child too. I hope you will consider reading on. I truly understand if you do not. I hope you will not be afraid of my words. Like I said before and will say again. This is the way I choose to go through my grief. May God bless you on your path.

Finding God In The Valley

It is so easy to find God on the mountaintops when everything is going the way you expect it to go. The view from the top of a mountain is breath taking. All you have to do is close your eyes and you can feel the warmth of the sun and smell the sweet smell of flowers in bloom. It is on the mountaintops you feel the security of who you are in God. It is on the mountaintops where you feel nothing bad can happen to you. Until one day, without warning, it happens. You find that you are no longer on that beautiful mountaintop but somewhere you have never been before. It is a place of total darkness with no light to show the way. It is not only dark, but it is very cold too. It is in this place of darkness and cold that every man will test his faith. Will you still believe when you can't find your way? Will you still believe when you are left there to find your own way out? It is easy for others to say have faith when they are on the mountaintop with a clear view of all things. It is easier to see the valley and know the way out from the top of the mountain then to live in the valley with no view of the top at all. I believe it is in the valley days. The days when you truly get to meet God on his terms. The God I knew on the top of the mountain is not the same God I am getting to know in this valley. In this valley where I live, I am getting to know the God who loves me no matter what. For the longest time I did not want to know him. I was so mad and full of anger. I am only now starting to know the new God I thought I knew so well before. The reason I am getting to know him now is I finally let go. You know the old saying, "Let go and let God"? Well that about sums it up. When you are in the valley you do not have much choice. You soon come to realize you are going to be in the valley anyway so why not let God. For me I just got tried of fighting it took to much energy and I finally gave in. That is not to say I got it now, far from it. It just means I realize I need Gods help to get me through this valley and not only get me through the valley, but to help me climb the mountain so I can once again have a view from the top. With the experience of knowing the valley is not that far away. The valley is the place to grow in God. The place where if you let it can open your eyes to a God that cannot be put in a box. To a God that is much bigger then you can imagine. To a God that loves all peoples regardless of stature, color, race or religion. He loves us all, and we will all come to know him in or own special way. We all have a valley waiting at the bottom of the mountaintop. No one can live forever at the top of a mountain and still grow in God without first going to the valley.

Good Grief

ood Grief. If that is not a play on word, then nothing is. Before I was on this side of grief, I never thought much of it. How could there be such a thing as good grief? Did you ever wonder where some phrases came from? I have. If I were to say Bad Grief not too, many people would pay much attention to me. So what would cause the word good behind something bad and somehow make it an okay word to say?

I would say, to say because saying something good behind something bad makes the bad thing seem better, or nicer, or more palatable.

It seems we cannot stand to tell it like it is. We have to always try and make it nicer, or better, or clean it up before we say it. What is wrong with just saying it the way it is? Does our saying it like it is, make it a bad word?

I know for me I always try to say it the nice way but in doing that I know I have cheated you out of the truth of it. Don't you think so? Doesn't everyone deserve the truth, even if it hurts? At least they know where they stand and can make a choice to except it, and then they can decide to stay or go. Not everyone wants to cover up or mask the truth.

If I were to take half the energy it takes to develop a dance around the truth or cover for what is really on my mind, I would be further down the road to self-awareness. I think I cheat people out of the real me when I am not totally honest. Why would I do this then is the real question? I think the reason I do this is because I am afraid. I am afraid that the true me, or real me will not be liked.

I really want to let the real person in myself out and let her fly or fall, and if she has to learn to fly again, and again. I would love to do what I do in the comfort of my own home when no one is watching wouldn't you?

How nice it would be to really have that freedom. So I agree you could say there is sometimes, such a thing as good grief. It is always good to tell about a person lost inside us all. Good grief! Can you believe I made it through this?

How Do You Shut Off Your Mind

How do you shut off your mind? When the rest of the world wants you to move on, how do you tell them you cannot shut off your mind? That it is impossible to shut off your mind. When the world asks me to move on, I shake my head and say how? How can I move on when all my mind sees is Ryan? I see Ryan hugging me. I see Ryan kissing me. I see him crying and telling me he has fallen down and wants me to comfort him. I see him snuggling next to me at night to go to sleep. I hear him laughing and giggling because he played a joke on me. I hear him calling me mommy. I hear him say I love you mommy. You are the best mommy in the world. I hear him say goodnight mommy I will see you tomorrow. Well, there is no more tomorrow for me with Ryan. There is an only yesterday. Yesterday is filled with Ryan. So when you ask me to move on you are asking a lot. You are asking me to leave him behind in yesterday and to come join you in tomorrow. I would love to move on into tomorrow. In fact, I am speaking to you from tomorrow you just didn't notice. You didn't notice because I am not the same person I was when I was in yesterday with Ryan. I am a new person trying to find my way here in this new day. I am trying to find my purpose and I am looking for the reason to go on.

What I notice the most about people, when they say I have to move on is this; they, never go to the next step. What I mean by that is they never thought before they say it, and put themselves in my shoes, and say to themselves, what if that were I? Would I be able to go on? Would I be able to move on if my child died? I know it is something people don't want to think about, and I know they don't even want to imagine it. If they can't even imagine it, imagine it being your reality. Imagine waking up every day to the reality that you are never going to see your child again. Imagine knowing you are never going to see him grow up become a man. Imagine all your hopes and dreams that you had for him and now do that with the understanding that he is lying in a grave. Do you think the next time you see me you could say to me it is time to move on? I don't think so! I honestly don't think you could.

What I would love for people to do when they see me is this; I want them to come up to me and grab me and say I can't believe you are here! God bless you for even having the ability to live another day without your child! God bless you for even taking another breath! God bless you for not losing your mind. I know people mean well, and don't always know what to say. I just thought I would write and tell you how it feels to hear people say: It is time to move on. I thought that by sharing how it is for me, it might make a difference the next time you see someone like me. I hope it would give pause you to think before you say the word move on. I hope it will give you insight to change the way you see a bereaved mom or dad. To see us as the different people we are, and not expect us all to be the same because our children have died. My hope is that you realize the need to treat the whole person and not leave out the grieving person. Grief isn't something you get over or recover from it isn't something you can put behind you. It is something you walk along with. Grief will be with me until I take my last breath on this earth.

I hope people will understand when I write this. I am not trying to say they don't care. Those of us that are grieving know it is difficult to deal with us. I am only trying to let you know what those words sound like from our point of view. How they hurt and sometimes make us angry. Other then wearing a sign there is no way we can let you know about our pain. Yes we will move on. We do it every day. We just don't want to hear people tell us to. We want to do it at our own pace, slow, and easy and a little at a time and try and feel our way back into a world without our child.

In Search Of

———⚜———

eep in the far-reaching corner of my soul, I scratch to find my humanity. I dig to explore a new universe, to go on an expedition to find who has survived this catastrophe. Has anyone survived? I unearth lots of remnants and pieces of a past life, a life now broken to bits from an event so powerful it shattered the previous one with such force it can't be found. As I look through the rubble to find some form from the past I discover a piece of the puzzle, just one piece. I know where I'm standing is a complete picture, but all I can see is pieces. I don't know where to start. I don't have the strength to start. I spend a lot of time looking through the pieces trying to sort them out and wondered what they were like. Did they feel like I do? Did they laugh like me, and cry like me? Were they trusting and curious, and want to know the meaning of life? My question is can something this broken be put back together and ever be the same? If I was a builder and came upon this mess I would see it as a challenge to start anew. I would look for the foundation, clear out all the rubble and start fresh. Take apart of the old and add the new. Hoping to create a building that was new, yes, but with great character and strength from it's past. To bring with it refinement something to be admired and respected for surviving it's past and coming out of it with grace and humility. Maybe I can learn to be a builder and start to rebuild from the foundation up keeping those things of value and add them to the new. You never know I might even like this new form, this new creation this new evolution, this new me.

Observing myself

As I look at myself today, I see many things. I see how I made it through another day without you. I see myself riding a giant wave that takes me very high and then brings me down very quickly. It moves so fast it literally take's my breath away. It is on these days it is very difficult to function without someone noticing the changes you go through. You want to just hide from the world on these days but sometimes you get sucked right in the middle of the world very exposed and raw with no place to hide. I hate these days! I just want to be invisible on days like this but if I can't be invisible, beige will do.

The thing that really amazes me is this: I have been on his path of grieving for almost four years now and on most days I do okay but on other days I feel like it just happened to me. I miss you so much. I don't think I will ever get over the missing you part. Today I miss you like you just left me. I feel like crying all the time. I just want to hold you and smell you again. I miss your laugh and the silly faces you use to make at me. I miss doing things with you. I miss growing with you. I still have a hard time believing you are gone and are never coming back. Today is just one of those days, I have to deal with. I love you and miss you today and always.

One of the hardest things for me to get use to is, trying not to feel guilty for being here when you are not. This is truly the hardest thing for me to get use too. How do you, as a mother make that okay in your head? People try to help you with this by saying things like; it isn't your fault. I know that in my head but my heart just won't buy it. How can any mother make peace with something like that? I know I will often reflect on this thought, especially when I go to that deep place I go and when I do go to that deep place I will fight my way back again. One thing I have realized now about going to that deep place is, I know I can find my way back because I have done it before.

When I go to that sad place for however long I do, I can feel real life happening around me but I can't seem to catch on to it at this time. I think the reason is, I don't want too! I also think this is my time with Ryan and if I let my life in, I lose my time with him and I can't feel him. If I had to explain what I feel like when I am there it is very much like the feeling I get on a rainy day when I stay in bed and pull the covers over my head to close the world out for a little while. It is like running away from the world but knowing it will be there when you return. It is taking a break! That's all it is. As I look at myself today, I see many things. I see how I made it through another day without you. I see myself riding a giant wave that takes me very high and then brings me down very quickly. It moves so fast it literally take's my breath away. It is on these days it is very difficult to function without someone noticing the changes you go through. You want to just hide from the world on these days but sometimes you get sucked right in the middle of the world very exposed and raw with no place to hide. I hate these days! I just want to be invisible on days like this but if I can't be invisible, beige will do.

The thing that really amazes me is this: I have been on his path of grieving for almost four years now and on most days I do okay but on other days I feel like it just happened to me. I miss you so much. I don't think I will ever get over the missing you part. Today I miss you like you just left me. I feel like crying all the time. I just want to hold you and smell you again. I miss your laugh and the silly faces you use to make at me. I miss doing things with you. I miss growing with you. I still have a hard time believing you are gone and are never coming back. Today is just one of those days, I have to deal with. I love you and miss you today and always.

One of the hardest things for me to get use to is, trying not to feel guilty for being here when you are not. This is truly the hardest thing for me to get use too. How do you, as a mother make that okay in your head? People try there hardest to help you with this. They may say a thing such as it isn't your fault. I know that in my head but my heart just won't buy it. How can any mother make peace with something like that? I know I will often reflect on this thought, especially when I go to that deep place I go and when I do go to that deep place I will fight my way back again. One thing I have realize now about going to that deep place is, I know I can find my way back because I have done it before.

When I go to that sad place for however long I do, I can feel real life happening around me but I can't seem to catch on to it at this time. I think the reason is, I don't want too! I also think this is my time with Ryan and if I let my life in, I lose my time with him and I can't feel him. If I had to explain what I feel like when I am there it is very much like the feeling I get on a rainy day when I stay in bed and pull the covers over my head to close the world out for a little while. It is like running away from the world but knowing it will be there when you return. It is taking a break! That's all it is.

Painting Words

When an artist paints a picture, he paints you his interpretation of what he sees. He paints from his soul. He takes everyday colors and paints them on a blank canvas.

Soon the picture starts to appear, and gives life to the feeling he has in his soul. It is the same for a writer only he paints the picture with words and the paper he writes on is his canvas.

The picture he paints depends on the depth of his soul he has tapped into. I paint my words as raw as I can to expose the very core of my pain. How can I tell you about my pain? How can I tell you what it feels like to lose a child and go on living? The truth is I can't. I can't because unless you have lost a child you could never truly understand my pain. I paint with my words as near as I can, and bring you like someone taking a tour through an art gallery. I take you picture by picture and let you draw your own conclusions. Sometimes the viewing is hard to take and you close your eyes so you can't see it. Just because you closed your eyes doesn't mean the picture is not there. It is just not there for you.

There are some people who would say why would you paint a picture like that? Why show the ugly side of life? Why didn't the artist paint a nice picture with pretty colors and nice scenery? It would be nice if that were the reality of life. Life is not always beautiful and there are times when the ugly side needs to be painted. How can we appreciate the beauty of life if we never see the ugly side and what would we compare it with? Many people tell me I should not stay in the place of rawness in my writing that I should write about the higher understanding of life. I wonder what they mean by that. Do they mean I should be untruthful and write about only good things and keep the raw ones to myself? Do they really want to live in a world so black and so white? I would prefer to paint with vivid colors, even though it can be shocking at times. At least it says I am alive.

Writing to me is a way to express the pain of losing my son and if by writing my pain it makes you uncomfortable I understand. I know it is not for everyone. But, there are people out there just like me who may not be able to express the pain that is deep inside of them. These people need to see that they are not crazy for feeling the way they feel and most of all that they are not alone in that feeling. This is the reason I write. I write to let them know they are not alone. Writing is like a picture. Sometimes it speaks to your soul and sometimes not. It is all in the eye of the beholder. So I must continue to write and express, and paint my picture with words regardless if you can see it or not. But, if you can see, and understand what I have written then I have done my job.

Perspective

I guess it all depends on perspective. It is all about where you are looking at it from and what angle. As I look at Ryan death now, I can see it so differently now. In the beginning when Ryan first died, I swore up and down, that I would not let this happen. What I mean by that is, I swore I would not let time steal my grief and pain over losing Ryan. I fought this with everything inside me.I remember even telling my doctor; do not think that by me coming here I am going to get over losing Ryan that will never happen. I will not let time take Ryan away from me. My biggest fear was that somehow by learning how to live without Ryan, I would somehow forget him. I could not imagine my life without Ryan in it, but here I am three years down the road I never wanted to go down and I am doing just that! I am living without Ryan. How did this happen is what I keep asking myself? Did I somehow manage to have something to do with it? I hope not.

Really, all it is is life going on. If you live and breath it is inevitable, it will just happen. If I ever had a doubt about life moving on after a tragedy, I do not now. I learned that the hard way.

I am now on a new road again. This road is a road I am looking forward to traveling down. It started out one way and now it has taken a turn down a part of the road we had not planned. I am truly putting all the new levels of my spirituality to the test. I purpose myself to think things through before I say a word when an issue comes up. I love having some kind of control over what I say and do. When I step back and do not react right away to a situation, the issue at hand presents itself in full and makes itself very clear, but if you react from your gut, first you never get to see it clearly.You just become reactionary and have to deal with the aftermath. I feel calmness in my sprit I never had before. I think what it is, is that Ryan's death taught me that nothing can shake me as bad as his death, anything after that doesn't seem to warrant getting that excited over. Now that is what I call true perspective. I could have done without that for sure. So, now that I have this new perspective about life, where do I go from here?

I know I have a lot of stuff inside me. I feel it. It is good stuff, I just need to find away to get it out and when I get it out, I want it to go somewhere. I want to be able to help others with what I have learned if that is at all possible. I feel that I am on a mission of some kind. I think if I just sit back, it will reveal itself to me. I want to make sure it is the real deal. I have learned a lot about patience on this road back to my sanity. I am in a completely new woe world that I helped build, although I hate to admit it, I did help. I made a choice and by making, the choice I helped to create this new world I now live in.

I think my world is more about acceptance. I have to learn how to accept this new world and me and to do it without feeling guilty about living again. I think I am doing a good job at that. I am starting to feel more comfortable every day. My hope is that a grieving parent who reads this might get some hope out of knowing that someday down the road this could happen for them or at least know that someone who is in the same shoes as them went down the road and got to a place like this. They can also know that even if they do not get to a place like this, it is okay too. Everyone deals with their grief differently, it is a private thing and very, very personal to the one grieving, and even another grieving parent can grieve differently then another one. My thought is to give permission to the one grieving to grieve whatever way they want. There is no right or wrong way to do it. This is your right as a grieving parent; let no one tell you how you have to do it. You earned that right the day your child died. I would dare anyone to tread on that ground. That is holy ground. Watch out tread carefully!

Profound State

I can never live life the same again. The value of everything has changed. It changed because I live in a profound state of mind. You can never look at life the same when you are coming from that place. I will forever look at life through Ryan's dying. When I look through Ryan's dying there can be no such thing as a normal every day emotion. When I look at children, I see Ryan in them. A rush of emotion sweeps over me that can't be described. It brings me to a place of remembrance that is so tangible I can smell it, see it, and touch it. Unbelievable Imagine gong through that all your life. Nothing will ever be simple again. I will miss that part of life, the simple part that is. Simple is what we all strive for. It is comfortable. It is relaxing it is sometimes nothingness. Oh, how I wish I could have some nothingness. Maybe if I did I would feel more real or feel like I am in this world without Ryan and it is okay! There is just to much pain inside of me for Ryan to ever do that. When I am not busy doing something in life and I'm with my own thoughts I feel sad, yes, but very safe there, maybe that's because Ryan is so alive there, or maybe it's because I do not have to bury him there. I am starting to realize that what I am feeling is as if I am moving through life with my clothes off! I feel very exposed and naked. When, in reality no one even notices. So, you see this profound state of mind that I'm in doesn't allow for simple ness or easygoingness. All the things I took for granted before. I now live in this complex place where everything is so intense, deep, and meaningful. I don't mind it most of the time but sometimes you just want to lay back and relax and say nothing much going on today. Just enjoying that for what it is: Nothing. Gone are the days of nothing

Returned Gift

One day I got this gift. At the time I got it I didn't appreciate just how beautiful it was. I became very busy with the everyday concerns of life and got use to it being there through it all. Like a lot of people you never stop to think of what you would do if it wasn't there. It never enters your mind. Until one day it happens. Something comes and says return to me the gift you have. It seems you have no need for it. It's apparent you don't see the value and treat it has if you can replace it, or return it, if it is broken or lost. It is then, and only then do you hold on to the gift and say no, you can't take my gift. It's mine.

Now that I know my gift is at risk of being taken from me I start to look at this gift in a way I never did before. The value increased right before my eyes. I looked and saw how so much of my life revolved around the gift. It was then and only then did I start to treat my gift in a way it deserved to be treated. I saw the wisdom the gift had and how I could learn from something I thought couldn't teach me, but I was to teach it. I saw things from a different perspective. I learned to look at the little things in life. This gift allowed me to visit my childhood and be a child once more and feel free to let go and be myself. The gift was not only a gift, but the gift gave a gift.

In order to have the gift there was one key thing you had to do. You had to receive the gift. Many people can get a gift but to get is much more different then to receive a gift. To receive is to take hold of and make part. The most important part of receiving a gift is to accept it. Acceptance says you are valued, you are home, you are comfortable, and you are at peace. So take this from someone who knows. Check and see if you have been overlooking your gift today before someone comes along and says. I've come to take your gift back. Please return it at once.

Speaking a different language

*L*ately, I feel like I am speaking a different language from the rest of the world. I don't know how to describe what this feels like except to say, it feels good most of the time but can be a very lonely feeling too. It is a lonely place because you feel separate from the rest of the world. You can feel isolated in your own thoughts.

I have often thought about, what this is I am doing when I write. I would question what it is, I am sharing and if I should share my thoughts. When I thought about it today, I found my answer. I would consider my writings an open journal or diary of my everyday thoughts. It is just me sharing, my process through life. Weather my own personal thoughts and feelings can help someone else, I am not sure. I figure I will just write them out and at least get them out, instead of letting them bang around the walls of my mind. I always feel so much better if I get them out.

When I am writing like I am right now, I feel so sensitive to my emotions. I am usually on the edge of feeling like I want to cry. This is the time I know I really need to write and get it out. Even though everything inside me really doesn't want to write, it just wants to get caught up in the emotion of the situation. It is this process that helps me to focus through the feeling. I am so glad I can write my feelings out. I don't know how other people get through it. I think I would have a very hard time if I couldn't get my feelings out. I think when I write them out and see them on paper it helps me to not only validate them but also to start the process of working through them.

This is where I feel like I am speaking another language. In my everyday living and dealing with people I have periods of feeling confused and my thought process doesn't always feel right. It is so different when I write. When I write all my thoughts come together without hesitation. I never seem to have a confusing thought. I don't know what it is about writing that helps me sort out my thoughts and feelings but whatever the process I am glad I have writing to help me. I love it so much. I could cry at the thought of how much I love it. Thank you God for the ability to write out my feelings. I really appreciate the gift you gave me.

I don't know what caused me to start writing today, except to say it was a feeling that felt like it wanted out. It needed to work its way out, like the birthing process. It starts and once it starts it has to finish. It has a beginning and it has an end. It also is painful but it is pain worth going through because it brings with it something new. The key is going through that process with that in mind and going through that with the idea that you are bringing something new out. A new thought or a new idea! You want to have gone through it for a reason. If I have to go through something emotional I want to go through it for a reason. I want to have grown from it. I would want to have learned something for all my trouble. I am always conscious of what is happening to me in an emotional way. I pay attention to what is happening to me on a daily basis.

There could be a problem when you start to think like this! The problem being you have to take responsibility for your thoughts and the way you answer them. Although this is the place you want to be, it is also the place you don't want to be. I know that sounds confusing but it really isn't. This is the place you strived to be in but I have often found myself wishing I were as dumb as they come. Sometimes I don't want to take responsibility for my thoughts or actions. I just want to let it go. Well that isn't possible once you have achieved this level in your spiritual growth. You can't go backwards once you have the knowledge. You can be stuck in the process but you can't go backwards once you have reached this level. This would be like saying I can't walk after learning how. You could just sit down and not walk but the ability to walk is always there. You can't forget how to walk once you have learned. It would take a physical injury to your body or mind to stop you from walking again.

The language, I am speaking now isn't always understood by others. Most people don't want to be bothered with the responsibility of acting on their thoughts. They would rather just stay in their own little world and stay focused on themselves. To search outside themselves for an answer isn't even in their realm of thinking. If you are to stay at this level you have to tell yourself that, not everyone in your life is going to understand you. It is in this place you have to be very careful who you have in your life.

The person who is in your life doesn't have to be in the same place but they better be traveling on a spiritual journey to enlightenment. If they are not you will find yourself very frustrated and lacking some kind of fulfillment and you will lose your peace of mind. You could even lose your serenity. So keep this in mind when you choose the people in your life. It is really to your advantage to have someone who doesn't totally think like you. This helps to sharpen you. It is like steal rubbing against steal. Sooner or later they cause each other to become sharp and know one even noticed it was happening. All of a sudden you noticed things were different. It wasn't really over night; it was actually a process that was happening from the very beginning, it was just very subtle. So it is a good thing to rub against each other. Of course this takes balance! The more you pay attention to yourself the more you will realize where the balance is. Don't be too hard on yourself at first. Just learn to go with the flow and not against it. Be very forgiving to yourself, it will help you to forgive others too.

What you are willing to do for others you should first do for yourself. You should practice being good to yourself first. Sometimes we forget to be good to ourselves and take care of our own needs. I don't know about everyone else but I often take care of others before myself. It isn't wrong to take care of others first in most cases.

The point I am trying to make is: not to do it in spite of yourself. It is here once again that balance is required. You have to know when to give to others and when not too. Giving to others is an honorable thing but you can't give to another if you are on empty. This is something I am working on myself, that's why I mention it. I am the worst offender of this! I need to listen to these words myself. Do you see how my writing isn't about, how I think I got it like that or how I think I know it all! It is about how I am learning as I write and I am hearing my words just like you are. I am just sharing my learning process with you as it happens for me.

I am always torn about whether I should share my thoughts or not when I get to a place like this. It is here and right now, that I am not sure what to do. So from here on out, I am writing my thoughts about my own personal process.

I don't know why I battle to have someone understand me. I question why? Why do I need someone to understand me now? What need am I trying to fulfill? Am I just throwing it out there to hear myself and then answer myself? Am I just trying to help myself by writing it out and reading it to myself? Well, whatever it is I am doing, writing it out seems to help me. It relieves me of the emotions I am feeling at the time I am writing it out. It feels like a giant weight is being lifted off of me. I feel like I can breathe again. It allows me to get a better perspective on how and what I feel.

I think the thing that bothers me the most is. I try with all I have inside me, to have an understanding for others and when I don't get that back, I have a hard time of it. This is when it takes everything inside me to try to rise above the situation. I really have to push myself pass this. My flesh is screaming out to be selfish. It wants so much to satisfy its own desire. It wants to say very low things. It wants to call attention to itself so bad. I can even feel it now as I am writing this. Thank God for me writing this out right now because I know the writing out process will help me rise to the level I need to be to get through this. The writing out process seems to dissipate any angry feelings I may be having.

As I end this piece, I can feel the peace of God coming over me. When this happens to me, it is like a rush or an emotional high. It is such a great feeling. I wish I could have this feeling all the time but then again you would never appreciate the good feeling if it were here all the time. I just want to end by saying; I love the process! I hope I always keep this in mind when I am going through different situations in my life. I pray God will always allow me to write out my feeling because when I do, I always come through my feeling with a better attitude and perspective on life. Writing gives me the ability to take a pause in my thinking and the benefit of that is, it gives me the time to rethink my response to the thought and more often then not it changes my reaction because it allows me to take the emotionalism out of my response.

What I would say to you is this: If you are not the kind of person that likes to write, then do the next best thing and stop! And take a deep breath and journey inward and find that place of peace, reflect on the thought for a while and soon you will realize you are not in the same frame of mind concerning the thought. The mind and your emotions speak two different languages. It is the language of life and we all need to learn it. All it takes to learn it we need to take a twelve inch trip from your mind to your heart and on the way there you will acquire a full understand for the language that is spoken there. I wish you well on your journey.

The Book That Never Ends

It seems that every time I try to end my book, I seem to be in another place in my process through grief. Each place seems different and most of the time a better place. I can feel myself growing all the time. My battle is trying to feel good as I process further down the road, without feeling guilty about where I am at. The way I move is by some how putting my grief in a place that is shut off from the rest of my emotions. I have to tell myself this is what I am doing, then once I have done that, I have to give myself permission to go on and not only go on but to go on with the joy for living. I am learning how to do this and feel comfortable at the same time. I want to feel good in my skin and at peace with myself. I wish I didn't have to make a decision about how to do it, I wish I didn't have to think about it at all. For those of us that have to grieve our children we must know we will be doing this the rest of our lives. It is all about choices. We can choose to stay stuck in places in our grief or we can choose to move on. It is this choice that is so hard. The rest of the world would agree that this is the right choice. I can understand their reason for their thinking like that; Of course it is the better choice but not necessarily the easier one for the grieving parent. To those that love us and care about us it is the choice that says to them you are okay and getting on with your life. It is in these times that your grief becomes very personal and private. It is here where you can't share anymore. To share in this place with someone who hasn't been through this kind of grief is pointless. To them is seems like you are making a choice and the choice you are making is to hold on to the pain. How do you explain that to hold on to the pain is really your attempt to hold on to your child? and that the pain is just the catalyst to do that.

I am learning more about the pain every day. The feeling of pain changes all the time too, as you process through grief. The pain I felt in the beginning is different then the pain

I feel today. The pain I feel today is more like a reminder, it serves as a gentle voice of my sub-conscious, letting me know or validating my experience. How do you tell the rest of the world that and if you did would they understand it? I think the biggest lesson I learned through my process through grief is this; In the beginning I wanted so much for everyone to understand me and my pain. I worked over time trying to get them to understand me. Why I did that I don't know. Now, as I look back I see I wasted a lot of energy trying to get them to understand me. It really isn't important for them to understand my pain. It is more important for me to understand why I needed them too. I think the hardest thing was hearing people say, you have to go on. God that use to get me so crazy! Of course I have to go on! And I choose that every day I decide to get out of bed and start my day. Going on is really the easy part. You just get up and go. You don't even think about it, you just do it. I am coming to an understanding I never thought I would and that understanding is: that sooner or later you just can't write enough about it and because grief is a process, a process that continues all the time. There really is no end to a grief book. It is a choice you make. You have to choose to stop writing, but just because you stopped writing, doesn't mean the process has ended, it just ended up to this point. The grieving parent is a walking grief book and that book has no ending, it just process's

The Difference

The only difference between choosing to live or to die is the ability to see tomorrow in today. I think when people are in the depths of the darkness today they did not have the glimmer of light for tomorrow. They just could not get out from under the pain of today to see the light. All they could see was the never-ending pain and sorrow that this day has bestowed upon them. Somehow in that darkness we have to push ourselves forward whether we stumble and fall or just reach inside ourselves for the strength to carry on. There will be days when we feel like we are in the endless nights of winter with no spring in sight. It will just be the brutality of the cold hard winter that brings with it stinging winds and frost.

It is in that cold dark place we live with the pain of losing our child. Somehow we must find a way to survive that place. This is where it gets tough. We ourselves must bring the warmth and light of a new day. It will take the action of our choice that we ourselves most reach down with everything we have got to pull out the very reason to go on. And it is in that pulling out process, we must find the sweet memories, and moments in times we have shared. Times filled with never-ending dreams and hopes of a future cut short. Most of all we must reach down and pull out the beauty that lies deep inside the ruins of a broken soul, the beauty of which has yet to be uncovered and discovered.

We must look for the light in every day no matter how dark it gets. Remember it only takes the light of one small candle to light a whole room. It only takes one flicker of light to dispel a heart full of darkness. So always keep the light of hope in your heart today because you never know it might be someone's torch for tomorrow that will light their path and lead them into their truth.

The Mountain

Some people climb mountains because they choose to. Some people because they have no other choice. My mountain came into view when my son died. Little did I know at that time how big, that mountain was?

The first day I approached the mountain, all I could see was the bottom and from that prospective I could not see the top and had no idea what lay ahead of me. A mountain does not look so scary from the bottom. I tried everything possible not to have to climb it. So, at first I stayed at the bottom, and very content to be there. I was not even thinking about climbing it. Why would I want to climb a mountain? I never had any training in mountain climbing before, so I pitched camp at the bottom to try and think of a way around it. That was my only thought. At night at the bottom I would busy myself with thoughts of yesterday. I would be content to travel back in time and relive my life, as I knew it. I got a lot of comfort from that at first and this seemed to work for a long time, until, one day I realized my life was not moving forward or going anywhere. So when morning came I made a decision to try and move on. I got up feeling pretty good. I was well rested from a good night's sleep and was as ready as I could be.

Soon dawn came I started out on my adventure. The first thing I did was walk around the perimeter of this big mountain to see if I could walk around it. I did that for at least a day and with no end in sight. Then, I once again pitched camp for the night. This happened for many days, with no evidence of the other side. That night at the bottom of the mountain reality was starting to work its way in. And the reality of that caused me to cry. I cried because I thought by now I would be on the other side. Moreover as I was starting to realize the possibility I was going to have to climb the mountain after all. I was never really prepared to have to actually climb the mountain. What would I need? How long would it take me? How would I survive were the questions I asked myself?

So when dawn came, I approached the mountain with that in mind and started my climb. I put one foot in front of the other, grabbing hold of anything to make the next move. After a long day of climbing, I found myself at a little landing and decided to make camp. The first night was very cold on the mountain, and all I had on was a light sweater, so I decided to curl myself up in a ball to keep me warm and fell fast asleep. I felt very alone on that mountain that night.

Soon is was daylight and time to start my climb again. I cannot tell you how long I was climbing for but I know it was for many days. There was this one-day in particular, I remember all I did was fall. I fell so much my knees were bleeding. And the more I fell, the angrier I became at this mountain. I did not want to climb it anyway! I was getting so angry that the anger cause me to look for a stick I could make a flag. The mountain was now becoming a challenge. I was determined to plant the flag on the top of that mountain and claim it for my very own. In the days to come, there were rain and windstorms and many a more cold night on the mountain. The harder it became the more determined I was to make it to the top. It was getting near to the end of my climb when I noticed something about the way I was climbing. I noticed it did not seem was so hard. I know the mountain had not changed, or had it? No! No, of course the mountain had not changed, how silly of me to even think that. A mountain cannot change. It was I, the person climbing the mountain that had changed. Little by little, I was fast becoming an experienced mountain climber but did not notice it. Before I knew it, I was able to climb with ease like I never had before.

Yes, it still was hard to climb on some days I just took my time on those days and did not fight the mountain. I took my cues from the mountain itself. Slowly but surely I started to come to the top. I will never forget the last days before I got to the top. I was getting my flag ready; I just needed to add one more thing. So I found a piece of charcoal and put my name on the flag I had so carefully made. I put it in my pocket to make sure to have it ready to plant when I reached the top today.

That last day of my climb, I climbed with great exhilaration. It was a day like no other! I was going to be king of the mountain! As I reached the top and lifted my head over, what I saw brought tears to my eyes and it took my breath away to see it. To my amazement and surprise there on the top of the mountain were hundreds and hundreds of flags blowing in the wind. And the thing that blew me away was, they all had names on them! Just like my flag did. It was then I broke down in tears because for the first time since I started to climb the mountain, I realized it was never my mountain at all! It was just mine that day, and tomorrow it will be someone else's. I thought the whole time I was climbing it, that no one has ever been here before. I now know the mountain is not just one person's mountain! And it wasn't just my mountain. It was just my mountain at that time. The mountain is everyone's. We just climb it at different times but sooner or later we all have to make the climb.

The Path of Grief

s I walk this path of grief, the one thing I would emphasize is this: Everyone has his or her own path or road through grief. Each person most honor where their at and how they feel. I hate when they use the word stages, as if you go through the stages in some kind of orderly fashion so that people can look and know and get a handle on just about where you are at before they start to apply pressure to you about getting on. So they can sit back and let time do the work. In the eyes of the griever, time can be not only your friend but also your worst enemy.

For me I have found this to be the most difficult part of my grief. I have found that writing was my way of getting through. I just sit and write down about a thought I'm having in that moment in time. Sometimes it is not pleasant to read, but if I'm to be honest I have to say it as it is in that very moment in time. Not too pretty it up with nice words and higher thinking. There are times I do have a glimpse of the bigger picture and can feel and understand my part in it. Then as if a big wind came and blew me off the top of the mountain I find myself back to earth and suffering that gut wrenching pain again and wondered how I could have thought those thoughts.

So, as I sit here and write and share, you will see not only the mountain top experiences but the very low valley ones too. I think my best writing comes from the heart of my pain. It comes from the times when reality is smacking me in the face. This book isn't about chapters. It is about pieces. It is about pieces of my moments through grief. It is also about birthing myself a little at a time. It is about one human being letting you peek at her soul and trying to give permission to anyone reading to feel what he or she feel no matter what anyone says. This is an invitation to visit my experience through grief and if by reading you should see yourself then at least you will know you are not alone.

Most of all, I want the one who is grieving to know I too, battle for my sanity every day. I live in the year, month, week, day, hour or second to second if that need be. I live wherever I have to be. It is in that moment-to-moment and second to second times that I do most of my writings. They seem to be the most unbearable ones for me. I often refer to them as "I'm coming out of my shin time" so I write instead. I write exactly how I feel. To some it would seem that you are digressing or going backward, when in reality you are doing exactly what your suppose to do. You are grieving. There is no right way or wrong way in my book. Just do it. Feel it. Tell it if you can.

Death never seems right for anyone, but the death of a child is never right and it is that very reason the death of a child is put in a whole other category where grief is concerned. It can't be compared to any other death. It just isn't right, and the battle we have, as griever's is what the rest of the world wants us to do is somehow make it right by going through the process like it was just another death. It can't be done. My hope is for those that read my words, whether you are a parent who lost a child or just someone who wants to understand those of us who have is just this. All the feeling we go through are our way of surviving an event in our lives that would destroy most people. We hear people say things like if it were I I would die. What are you saying to us when you say such a thing? Of course, we want to die at times when the pain is too much. Of course we want to end the pain, but then we think of our children, especially the ones who suffered a long illness and say, how could we give up when our children fought so hard to live? A catch 22 wouldn't you say? So what I have here is just pieces of myself split seconds in time with so much unsaid, so much more needing to be said and so much intangible left in the air.

I hope you can find some comfort and understanding for where you are at and that being right where you are supposed to be right here with me.

The Place That Never Ends

When I write I find that I am freeing myself to go to a world that lies deep inside me. It feels like I am jumping out of a plane and sailing in the sky with no gravity to keep me in place. It is the best feeling in the world. I love to write because it affords me the freedom to say what never comes to mind. It allows me to visit the deeper places of my soul. When I go there, I can once again become the child and speak the language that has long since been forgotten. I can once again speak the secret codes that will give me entry to places locked and forgotten. I can once again have the freedom to explore the endless sea of memories of a childhood revisited. I can once again, run with the wind in my hair and smell the sweet smells of flowers in bloom. Oh, what a wonderful feeling of freedom I get when I start to write. I can say all the things I never got a chance to say before. I can create a world of my own making. I can control who comes into my world and who does not. It is, I, alone who make the settings and writes the scripts. I give all the characters their voices. I can always be who I truly am. When I go to that place deep inside of me I find you there with your arms wide open, waiting for me to come join you. I see your eagerness to start the day. You have so many things to tell me and you do not have enough time to get it all out. You want to show me the new things you have discovered while I was gone. Such excitement in your voice it makes me feel like I have to hurry too. I have so many secrets to share with my best friend. God life is so beautiful in this place. Nothing bad can happen here. Only good things are allowed in this place. It is a well-guarded place with very tall walls. In the middle of this well-guarded place is a garden with every flower you can think of. It is the place of the never-ending sun. It is the land of forever after. It is the place dreams are made of. Gently I lie down in the middle of the garden with you to look at the sky to find the clouds are telling us a story as we watch them roll by. You share with me your dreams of being the ringmaster in a circus and a lion tamer too. I tell you how it feels to fly and touch the stars that are in the sky. I love this place I have deep inside because I know I can always come here when I am sad and want to cry. This world that lies deep inside is only for children that want to hide. The children that come here are all my friends. They like this place that never ends

The Transported Soul

I feel like my soul has been transported from a beautiful place filled with sunlight and laughter to a place filled with darkness and no sounds of childhood. It is a place that has me wondering around looking for something familiar, something with you in it. It is a place that has me calling out your name, and saying where are you? Please come out? This place is not a place I want to be but I cannot seem to find my way out. I feel like screaming someone please take me out of here I've had enough. As I spend time in that place I realize no one is coming to take me out of here. I am on my own in this place. I know I have to learn to survive in this dark place. I battle everyday for the courage to face the darkness with all its traps. It is like walking in a mind field. I remember the days when this very place was filled with the brightest of sunshine and the sounds of laughter could be heard everywhere. I remember when your smile alone warmed my heart and the look from your eyes gave me the hope of tomorrow. I remember when you shared your heart felt secrets with the utmost confidence, knowing they were ours alone never to be spoken.

I know it will take along time for light to totally enter this place. I know it will be me who will slowly let the light in. It is time, and time alone that will do the work because there is no way I can do the job alone. I will need help to light this dark place. I will need the help of God to show me the way in the darkness, until there be light once again. I will never see this place the same again. It will always be different for me. I must somehow see the difference and make peace with it. I must somehow understand the difference and make it my friend and invite it to my new home. It is a place that is very different, yet very much the same. The only difference is that you are not there.

Turning Inward

The act of turning inward is a choice to remove all the distraction from your life. When you choose to go inward, you choose to leave the outside world just where it is. You leave it outside of you. You know you are there when even though it would look like your world is crazy and upside down, you somehow manage to find peace in the middle of it. It is a peace that defies understanding and even has you questioning how this could be true.

This is finding your center or your place of balance. You will recognize that you are in this place because it is a place of comfort and gives you the feeling of security. You do not know why you feel so secure you just know you do. It is at this time you have to say to yourself, I know I do not have the total understanding and that is alright. I do not need to know it all right now. As long as I feel this feeling that is good enough for now. The understanding will come later, do not worry or stress about it, just relax in it. Sometimes I think we analyze things too much. We do not know how to just let it be. We always feel we have to be doing something or think about something. Why do we feel this way? What is wrong with sitting in silence? I know for me I use to have a problem with silence. I could not stand it. I finally know how to sit in my own thoughts.

If a thought comes in that I do not like it or is negative thought. I just dismiss it. I do not let it stay in my mind.

I only allow positive thoughts to stay. I do not have control over what comes in but I can certainly have control over what stays. I do not know why it took so long for me to get it, but I do now for some reason get it. I guess it just it happens when you are ready. I know, I am ready for this in my life now. It is the thing I worked towards all my life. It is a journey, a journey to find myself. I am in a place right now in my life, that I want to give. I want to give care and compassion to the one I love. I want to enhance and elevate and rise above myself and see the needs of the one I love. I want to be selfless and by being selfless truly give to myself. I know that sounds contradictory but in reality it is not. That is what true love is all about. It thinks of the other person first. It does not think of self first. That is selfish love. I want nothing to do with that kind of love. The love that is true love thinks of the other person first and puts it's own needs second. When you do that you give out of yourself and it never returns void. It always brings back with it all you have been looking for. It does this because it was in your act of giving, that it brought it back to you. That is a universal law, that you or I have no control over. I only wish I could have learned this sooner but if it happened sooner maybe I would have missed it. So all I can say is, I am glad I have it now. Now is where I am at and now is my time to grow and understand and give from my place of understanding. I will give from this place I am in right now because by my giving, I know I will receive and in return get the best of my love.

Changes happen in our life and we think we caused them to happen. Yes, it is true we made a choice or a decision to make a change but we don't always know what the result of that change will be. We have an idea of the end result but don't always have the knowledge of what road will get us there or what will be there down that road. Sometimes things won't go the way you expected them too. Well, when that happens we just need to take a deep breath and let God show us the way, and he will, if we let him. Just ask and wait and watch what he does. I know I should not be amazed at what he does yet I always find myself amazed and feeling guilty for not having believed in the first place. The biggest lesson I learned concerning God is patience. If we learn to wait on God, he will show us the way. I know this is a hard thing to do. For me it was always the hardest. I was always running way ahead of God and never giving him the chance to show me. It took me a while but I finally learned how to do that. Now when things happen, the first thing I do is say to me. Okay, what's happening here, this isn't what I planned on? Then my next thought is, okay God I know you have it all in control, I just need to sit back and wait on you to show me. That's the hard part. The waiting on God part that is, I say this because If we wait on God and do not become impatient it usually works out in our best interest.

This is what we have to keep in mind when we are going through something we are not sure of. He will make it known to us if we wait on him.

Welcome Home

It is like the wind. It is invisible. You can feel it and yet you cannot see it. In it's infancy let us say it is a breeze like. It can be calming, but like a wind in a storm, the forces can be destructive. When it comes, it comes over you like a great title wave pulling you up by your roots and causing a feeling of confusion and then you become like a human boat without a rudder. Rudderless the winds blow you from one unknown place to another. Now is the time to make decisions. Will this be an adventure to the center of you or will it be an unguided tour through the land of missed opportunity? And being waywardly bound you are grabbing at anything along the way to bring you stability. You are reaching outside yourself for the anchor that is within. Soon the winds will die down. And the seas will calm and it will be like there was never even a storm. My question to you is what has the storm taught you? Will you still seek to find the anchor in the calmness of the day? It doesn't make a difference whether you're in the calm of the storm or the storm itself. You have to have an anchor. You can drift in the calm as much as in the winds of a storm. The movement is just less notice. This in reality is more dangerous. You are unaware of its subtleties.

In reality, your soul is the rudderless boat. It has many different anchors, through its travels to find itself. All anchors serve the purpose of holding something fast or to keep it in place. However, not all anchors will cause you to grow in your soul=s journey to discover the meaning of the anchor.

What purpose does the anchor have besides keeping it in place? Can you have movement and anchor at the same time? Many people would tell you that it is not possible to have anchor and movement at the same time.

Many would ask, how could one have movement and still have an anchor at the same time? Truly, this is only possible if you step outside the mind of the normal thinking and keep in mind this: You are the Anchor and the anchor is you. And soon you will see somewhere along the way. You no longer had a need for the boat. What I really am trying to say is this.

We fight so hard to keep the boat afloat and miss the travel and the sights along the way. The place we traveled really was not such a strange trip at all. It is a trip, not too many people want to take. It is short in length, if you go direct. The Trip is, are you ready? Do you want to go? Well then let us go. You are now, on your way to your mind. It is a trip which is really the journey through, your heart. I thought you would never get here. Welcome home.

Who am I?

I often find myself having trouble explaining my feelings about my grief and what it means to me about the death of Ryan. I find myself at a loss for words most of the time. I do not know why I feel such a need to convey what this feels like? Maybe it is because I feel so confused most of the time about Ryan's dying and what it has done to me? And it effects my belief in who am I? And what I am after such a traumatic event.

These are the questions, I keep asking myself. I feel like I am so many people as I go through the grieving process. I feel that I am all different people and yet I am the same. I am connected and yet I am separate.

Sometimes, I can see all the different people in me and understand them and how they feel, sometimes they are angry! Sometimes I see them as sad and lonely people. I can see them and they are very deep, and are too afraid to come up to the surface because they know no one will understand them.

It would take to much trouble to explain this to people so I never talk about it to others. I can feel all these things happening to me. I can see the many changes in my moods. I know it is happening but I cannot stop it! I do not know if I would stop it if I could. How do I explain to someone how this feels? How can you tell someone and make him or her understand?

I guest the best way to describe it is to ask, how can you describe color to a blind man. You have known the rainbow and know how beautiful it is and yet you cannot share it with him. How frustrating that can be?

On the other hand, you have seen a sunset or sunrise and cannot experience it to him. Moreover the other side of that, which is the dark side the not so pretty sides of color that leave you empty, and sad.

I think what I am looking for is some kind of understanding for myself. I think if I can make others understand then somehow I will understand too if that is at all possible. I need to know who I am. Who I was, and who I will become.

Most people have that understanding throughout their lives. I have always struggled with this one. I was never sure about who I was, because I felt like more than one person sometimes. And Ryan's death has now opened me up to that thought again.

What made me feel more confused was how strong I felt about who I was at the time. I was very strong in character. So why would I have doubts? I always felt like I had a good mind and had an understanding of myself and yet there would be times I felt so called weak in my mind. How can I know myself when I cannot understand who I am?

This is why I feel the need to explain what this feels like. It feels crazy and sad. It feels happy and angry. It feels lost and found. It feels here and yet not here at the sometime.

It is every emotion all at once and then again very separate. It is beginnings. It is endings. It is ups and it is downs. I just want to know in all of this. Is there a me that can be found? Is there a me in there somewhere that is all together and not separate. Is there a me that does not feel strange but at home with herself. Does she feel comfortable with herself and does she feel at peace and not doubting who she is? Does she feel proud of herself and is she without a doubt? Does she feel she has to ask for approval or permission? Is she confident in herself? This is what I want understood and recognized without asking. This is the me, I truly want to be. The one that can stand there and tell you just exactly how she feels. This is the me I hope to become. This is the me that needs to be set free.

Poems section C

Broken People

Have you ever seen a broken person? What does that person look like? How many broken people are there in the world? I would bet more than you can possibly imagine.

I am a broken person and many people walk by me every day and do not notice. The reason they walk by me is because my broken-ness is not visibly. My broken-ness is on the inside. It is hidden from view of the world. But because it is on the inside, and you cannot see it, does that make me any less broken? What do I have to do for someone to notice it? Do I scream and yell? Do I cry out to them and say, look at me! Can you not see my pain? What do I have to do to get people to recognize something is missing from my life?

If, I could talk to them this is what I would say. I am a broken person! And I will always be a broken person and nothing will ever change that. Yes I will look like the real thing and act like the real thing, but underneath I am put together with spit and glue. I am very fragile in my emotions now and anything you say or do can set my day spinning. Although I look like everything is all right on the outside and you would not think so, by what you see. I am just one of the many broken people in the world trying to make it through. I want you to know my broken-ness comes at a very heavy price. It came for me at the death of my son.

When he died I felt like I would be broken forever and I would have to put myself back together and at the same go through the grieving process. I had to try real hard to hold myself together when everything inside was broken. Do you have any idea how hard that is? The world does not have much patience when it comes to broken-ness. It does not want to know anything about it. It would rather walk by it and pretend it does not see it. Because to say you see my broken-ness is to say you see my pain. And for you to have to say you see my pain is to be confronted with sharing my pain, and to share my pain is to say this could be me and believe me not too many people want to go there. They would rather keep walking and say, please God do not let this be me. Please! Please!

Brave are the people who are willing to see my broken-ness and very brave are those who are willing to see my pain but the bravest of them all are the people willing to share my pain and be my friend in that broken place.

Gone

One, are the days when I wake up and the day is new. Gone are the days when I would listen for your little feet as they hit the floor to start the new day's adventure. Gone are the days when you and I cuddle on a Sunday morning and tell each other how much we love each other. Gone are all the wonderful questions about life and the entire why questions of it. Gone too are those beautiful eyes I looked into and I could see all the answers to all my questions because they were right there in you. Gone are all my hopes and dreams of seeing you as a man, and seeing you as a father, and being someone's best friend. Gone! Forever are the times I will see you grow, or get new shoes, or see the latest rug rat movie or to taste the newest Gatorade. Gone are all the moments I will ever get to hold you when you cry because someone did a mean thing, or when you have fallen and just needed a hug. Gone forever is the sound of your voice when you call me mommy and gone forever is my life, as I once knew it. The life that was so full of you is gone. Gone forever is my baby, my boy, and my son. Gone forever is a piece of this mother's heart he took the day he died. Gone forever is the way I look at life. Gone forever is the way I feel about people, the way I think about God. And here to stay, is a mother who was blown out of her box where she lived and whose values have changed forever and here forever is a broken mom trying to piece herself back together and wondering whom this new person will be. Gone forever are the old, and here forever making the new. Here forever learning to live in life without you.

Good Grief

ood Grief. If that is not a play on word then nothing is. Before I was on this side of grief, I never thought much of it. How could there be such a thing as good grief? Did you ever wonder where some phrases came from? I have. If I were to say Bad Grief not to many people would pay much attention to me. So what would cause the word good behind something bad and somehow make it a okay word to say? I would say, to say because saying something good behind something bad makes the bad thing seem better, or nicer, or more palatable. It seems we cannot stand to tell it like it is. We have to always try and make it nicer, or better, or clean it up before we say it. What is wrong with just saying it the way it is? Does our saying it like it is, make it bad? I know for me I always try to say it the nice way but in doing that I know I have cheated you out of the truth of it. Don't you think so? Doesn't everyone deserve the truth, even if it hurts? At least they know where they stand and can make a choice to accept it, and then they can decide to stay or go. Not everyone wants to cover up or mask the truth. If I were to take half the energy it takes to develop a dance around the truth or cover for what is really on my mind, I would be further down the road to self-awareness. I think I cheat people out of the real me when I am not totally honest. Why would I do this then is the real question? I think the reason I do this is because I am afraid. I am afraid that the true me, or real me will not be liked. I really want to let the real me out and let her fly or fall. She may even have to learn to fly again and that's okay too. I would love to do what I do in the comfort of my own home when no one is watching. How nice it would be to really have that freedom. So I guest you could say there is sometimes a good grief. It is always good to tell about a person lost inside us all. Good grief do you believe I made it through?

I lent it voice

*lend it voice. It grumbles. It spits and snarls. It digs its heels in preparing itself to pounce at any moment. It violently shakes the tree to make it fall; And fall it will on a silent ear as if deafness could lessen the sound. It has no hands or arms or legs to run from it. There is no escaping the realness or the truth of it. The only redeeming feature is a friend called denial that ushers in at the most painful moment for a quick getaway to the island of dreaming.

Although, someday the voice will give up its rudimentary sound and bring up as if it had vomited a poison from the far-reaching depth of the soul. The vomiting causes it to cleanse and prepare for healing and quieting to bring with it peace and understanding. The voice lend most speak truth no matter how it sounds. If a sound isn't heard is there still a sound? Or can there be no sounds unless heard. Can you tell me what sound voice has? Or does voice have sound? This is a thought to be pondered. But you can only ponder it for a little while because it will lose its value. You must say it, feel it, hear it, and then move on. You must reflect, but never live in it. To live in it would bring confusion. It was never, meant to be kept in place. It was meant to express with no identification. It was meant to be free of attachments to a person. It was meant to be accepted on face value alone and with no explanation necessary and none to be given.

I see you Mommy

———◦⊱✿⊰◦———

$\mathcal{I}$ see you mommy when no ones there. You think I am not looking but I amThere! I can see your sadness and I feel so bad! I love you mommy I wanted to say I wish I could take all your pain away. When you are sleeping mommy, I take your hand and brush your forehead with a kiss. It is then I softly whisper how much you are missed. I tell all the others here what a great mom I have and how she battled bravely with all the things, I had! She is the best mom in the world. I would not change a hair. The only thing that, I would change, if I had it all to do. I would make her smile the way she always used to do. And if, I had to leave heaven to make her smile again I would do it in a heartbeat just to let her see me again. And if God would close his eyes, just for a second or two I would do it all for her just to make it true. I would like to tell my mommy that I really am okay. Moreover, that heaven is my home now and I really want to stay. Someday we will be together. I know it seems so long but I promise you mommy I will be happy all the time I am gone. There are so many things to do here. I am busy every day. I have no cancer here to rob me of each and every day. So my mommy, can you do me a favor? I hope it is not too much to ask. Please smile for me and do not be sad. I know this will be hard but please remember mommy I will always be near. When you go to sleep tonight just know that I am their softly planting kiss' in your beautiful hair. I love you mommy. I will never forget you. You are my only love, my best girl until we meet again.

Your loving son,
Ryan.

In a Smile

Remember the days when all you could afford to give away was a smile? And when you did what came back was worth so much more. It was that indescribable feelings of knowing you were right there in the middle of that smile.

The amazing part to me is how something so very simple and carefree, something that doesn't take a lot of thought at all to produce can cause such healing and warmth. How it can light up a dark room and show all those who are there where the door to happiness and contentment are. It can bring you down the road that leads to the mountaintop where the view alone says all things are possible if you believe.

It says come. Come light to this sad world filled with hopelessness and fear. Come light. Come melt the ice off the hearts of those who would call this a cold cruel place of sadness and unbelief. Come smile. Come and grab us when we least expect it. It is then and only then have you truly completed your mission. The unexpected smile is a five star smile. Nothing can hinder its effect. There is no time to find a defense against it or ward off its subtle impact on your downtrodden spirit.

There is no end to its depth and it imparts its warmth to the bottom of the soul. It is soulful because that is where it is from. Where it was born and now so readily returns. People say it is worth a million or you have a million-dollar one but in reality you couldn't buy one with gold much less afford it if you could.

A smile is just this; it is a heaven-sent jewel from God. The way to get one is to give one. So why not become the riches person in the universe. Start giving away smiles. You never know when you might get one back.

Little Boy in Blue

ittle boy in blue so strong and wise Are you happy there on your magic carpet ride?

Are your days filled with laughter as you sail across the sky? I can See you chasing moonbeams and putting them in a jar, and once again you throw them just to see how far.

Little boy in blue you are in our father's hands and he will loving take care of you until you are a man. He will show you the entire universe. The stars, the sun the moon and how so much a part of him is deep inside of you. So you see little boy in blue you have the answer to all your questions. You have the Key to every door. You have no mystery to solve just places to explore you have all the puzzle pieces not one missing Any more. The only thing that is missing from all the things I said is a piece of this mother's heart he took the day he died. And forever will he hold it and plant it in the sky so if you ever take notice of a night that is so clear think of all the Mother's heart's that are so very near.

Okay

What is okay? What does it say concerning you? Does it mean its okay that you are dead, or okay that you are not here living life to the fullest? I am having a hard time with that word today. I just cannot seem to get it in my language and to make it a part of my everyday conversations. God, I hate the word okay today. Because for me it could never be okay that you are gone, still I find myself saying that word for lack of another word that states what I really feel.

To replace the word okay, I would have to explain too much in a short period of time. More over who wants to listen to a mom talk about her dead child? I wish I did not have to say the word okay today. I wish I did not have to say okay because to say that makes me feel like I somehow managed to live when you died. I somehow managed to survive what; I thought could not be survived. I hate the word okay! I hate it because it is such a nothing kind of word. It is a word filled with no emotion at all. It is a word that has no human qualities. It is a word that makes no sense when you think about it. It is such a no word kind of word. It is just a word you stick in there to fill a space to take up the slack in a nonsense conversation.

A lot of things changed for me since your death the simple conversations I once used to participate in no longer have any value. Life has become more complicated for me now, which means, I have no tolerance for small talk or unimportant things. When this happens to you, life has a way of leaving you out in the cold as far as the rest of the world is concerned.

Where are you going find a place in a world where only meaningful conversations are taking place all the time? So for myself, I would rather isolate myself in my own world and have no conversation at all, except the one that is going on in my head. And this can be a very lonely place.

This is really going to be hard trying to get back into life's stream after such a devastating loss. I somehow have to find my way back and not only find my way back but to once again fit in when I get there. How can I ever fit without you? How can I ever live without you? How can I ever sing, or dance or feel joy again without you? How can I say the simplest word like okay and really mean it? Can you tell me why that is not okay? Because for me, it could never be okay again.

The Color of Grief

This is the journey to find the color of grief. It is a journey, that has a beginning but it has no end. So let us start out on this journey together to find the color of grief.

When I started out on this journey to find the color of grief, I had, no idea what to bring with me? This is a journey I have never taken before and I was not ready for this journey and was caught off guard. Could someone, please be my guide and help me get started. In the beginning of my journey to find the color of grief I feel myself walking through what I would describe as a very black place. There is not much light here in this place and I cannot find my way almost all the time on this journey to find the color of grief. I find myself having to rest almost all the time. I am so very tired and I am up-set because I did not find the color today. I hope maybe tomorrow I will find it. As I lie, resting and I fall off to sleep to only dream of what this color could be. If only I could find it! Or moreover, I could see it and maybe I could then understand it. I could find and somehow figure what it is and where it came from and why. Before you know it I am up again and once again, I am on the journey to find this color of grief. I do not understand why is it so hard to find? It is at this point on my journey that I ask God for help. I questioned God and asked him why I am having so much trouble finding the color of grief? Please tell me! God's answer to me was this: How can a color express your feelings? What would the color of high be? Tell me in a color the heights of it! How about the color of decent and depth? Describe to me that in a color. So to describe grief as a color there is only one way to do it. I would have to first tell you it has no color that you can see. Let's call the color of grief invisible, let's say it is see through because it is very clear for those who are experiencing it. Nobody can see the color of the pain that is on the inside. They can only see what you show them.

Nobody can see the depths of your loneliness. Nobody can see the aching in your heart. So what would you say the color of grief is? I think the best way to express grief in a color is, to see it as a rainbow of feelings. All of the feelings are important and necessary for the one grieving process. Moreover, if one of the colors is missing you have lost an important part of the rainbow and most importantly when one of the colors is missing you can never truly appreciate its complete beauty.

The Eye That Can See is still blinded

The eye that can see and is still blind is the saddest of all eyes, because it is the seeing eye that can walk right pass a hungry man with his hand out waiting for a mere few cents to put together to buy a cup of coffee or a piece of bread. It is the eye that can see that can look right past an old woman's hollowed eyes as she reaches for something to stable herself before she sits on a street corner, weary from the day of walking in circles and getting nowhere fast. It is this kind of blindness that is the worst of all. It is this kind of blindness you seldom regain sight from. It is man's inhumanity to mankind. If we could think for just a moment that this could be you, or me, or someone we love, could we just walk by? It is as if we not taking notice made it untrue or like it wasn't really there. But if the truth be known, it is us we are walking by. Yes, it is us, or someone we love. Do not think because you did not take notice that it changed the fact that they were there. They were there. And in spite of your turning away, they were there bigger than life itself and you just walked by. I am not saying this to you alone. I am saying it to myself too. We all at times, maybe more times than we would like to remember, have walked by like they were invisible or we were somehow momentarily blinded. It's a part of us; no one wants to take a look at. It is the ugly side of our humanity. The side we do not want to see. It is the side of us that is blind sighted. The only way to recover from this kind of blindness is to peel back the cover we have over our hearts. And let the light of love show us the way. Let the light of love reach down deep into our hidden pockets of gold, waiting to give of us to another, not in only a monetary way, but in a spiritual way too. It is to give hope by reaching out your hand in kindness, to offer not only material things, but to give of yourself in a kind word or smile. These things our much needed for the soul to survive. Not only theirs, but yours. So make a decision today to open up your heart and allow the gift of love in to peel back the blinder on your heart and let the light of love guide you to your kindness tomorrow. You never know you might be helping yourself.

The Key

As I live each day without you, I find I am living in a world I never known before. I am like an explorer setting out on a new horizon. I wonder about the mysteries that lie ahead of me. For the most part, it is very scary not knowing what is ahead of me. I like the feeling of safety common ground gives me. Walking in uncharted territory is not something I like to do. I am a very rooted kind of person but your death has taken me out of that place forever. Your death has changed the course of my life. So I sit here and say to myself I have two choices, either I stay in this place where I am at and live deep inside myself and keep everyone out, or I move on with the pain and forge new territory. I choose to move on because I know this is what you would want me to do. I know you would want me to go on with my life. I never in my life thought I would ever be in a place that has no place for you. Your death has created a key. It has created a key to unlocked doors I never traveled through before. It is the very key to my soul. It is the key that opened up the many different parts of me. One part is like a room filled with children's dreams and imaginings, and another filled with friends I never knew existed. They were all there behind locked doors. They were always there waiting to be part of me. They were always there I just never noticed them. They are now coming to me with open arms and hearts filled with love for me. They tell me to come play with them and be a part of them, and join in on the wonders of life. They echo songs of my younger days when life was so carefree. They tell me life is to be lived; do not stay in that sad place that locks the doors to life. They tell me not to stay in that dark place with no light of a new day. They tell me not to close my heart and let it wither like a rose on a vine. They tell me not to shut the window that lets in a summers breeze to cool me from the heat of day. They say, please do not lock us out of your heart and throw away the key.

The Mountain

ome people climb mountains because they choose to. Some people because they have no other choice. My mountain came into view when my son died. Little did I know at that time how big that mountain was. The first day I approached the mountain, all I could see was the bottom and from that prospective I could not see the top and had no idea what lay ahead of me. A mountain does not look so scary from the bottom. I tried everything possible not to have to climb it. So, at first I stayed at the bottom, and very content to be there. I was not even thinking about climbing it. Why would I want to climb a mountain? I never had any training in mountain climbing before, so I pitched camp at the bottom to try and think of away around it. That was my only thought. At night at the bottom I would busy myself with thoughts of yesterday. I would be content to travel back in time and relive my life as I knew it. I got a lot of comfort from that at first and this seemed to work for a long time, until, one day I realized my life was not moving forward or going anywhere. So when morning came I made a decision to try and move on. I got up feeling pretty good. I was well rested from a good nights sleep and was as ready as I could be. Soon it was dawn and I once again started out on my adventure. The first thing I did was walk around the perimeter of this big mountain. I walked around it to see if I could make away around it. I did that for at least a day and with no end in sight. Then, I once again pitched camp for the night. I did this for many days, with no evidence of the other side. That night at the bottom of the mountain reality was starting to work its way in. And the reality of that caused me to cry. I cried because I thought by now I would be on the other side. Moreover as I was starting to realize the possibility I was going to have to climb the mountain after all. I was never really prepared to have to actually climb the mountain. What would I need? How long would it take me? How would I survive were the questions

I asked myself? So when dawn came, I approached the mountain with that in mind and started my climb. I put one foot in front of the other grabbing hold of anything to make the next move. After a long day of climbing, I found myself at a little landing and decided to make camp. The first night was very cold on the mountain, and all I had on was a light sweater, so I decided to curl myself up in a ball to keep me warm and fell fast asleep. I felt very alone on that mountain that night. Soon is was daylight and time to start my climb again. I cannot tell you how long I was climbing for but I know it was for many days. There was this one-day. I remember in particular, that all I did was fall. I fell so much my knees were bleeding. And the more I fell the angrier I became at this mountain. I did not want to climb it anyway! I was getting so angry that the anger cause me to look for a stick I could make a flag. The mountain was now becoming a challenge. I was determined to plant the flag on the top of that mountain and claim it for my very own. In the days to come, there were rain and windstorms and many a more cold night on the mountain. The harder it became the more determined I was to make it to the top. It was getting near to the end of my climb when I noticed something about the way I was climbing. I noticed it did not seem was so hard. I know the mountain had not changed, or had it? No! No, the mountain had not changed, of course not how silly of me to even think that. A mountain cannot change. It was I! The person climbing the mountain that had changed! Little by little, I was forced and fast becoming an experienced mountain climber but did not notice it. Before I knew it, I was able to climb with ease like I never had before.

Yes, it still was hard to climb on some days I just took my time on those days and did not fight the mountain. I took my cues from the mountain itself. Slowly but surely I started to come to the top. I will never forget the last days before I got to the top. I was getting my flag ready; I just needed to add one more thing. So I found a piece of charcoal and put my name on the flag I had so carefully made. I put it in my pocket to make sure to have it ready to plant when I reached the top today. That last day of my climb, I climbed with great exhilaration. It was a day like no other! I was going to be king of the mountain! As I reached the top and lifted my head over, what I saw brought tears to my eyes and it took my breath away to see it. To my amazement and surprise there on the top of the mountain were hundreds and hundreds of flags blowing in the wind. And the thing that blew me away was, they all had names on them! Just like my flag did. It was then I broke down in tears because for the first time since I started to climb the mountain, I realized it was never my mountain at all! It was just mine that day, and tomorrow it will be someone else's. I thought the whole time I was climbing it, that no one has ever been here before. I now know the mountain is not just one person=s mountain! It was in fact never my mountain at all but more like it was every man's mountain we just climb it at different times but sooner or later we all have to make the climb.

The Whirlpool

—◦❦◦—

Grieving to me is like a whirlpool that comes and goes. One minute you can be in this quiet still place when out of nowhere it hits you. You feel yourself start to spin out of control. Down, down, down you go helplessly caught up in the momentum of the whirlpool itself. It is during this time you feel like you will never get out and you couldn't possibly survive. You feel like you cannot grab onto anything because it is all spinning out of control. There is really nothing you can do when this happens except to go with the flow. It is at this time, you do not want to waste your energy fighting nature it will only prove to frustrate you. Sooner or later the whirlpool will ebb and you will once again be in the calm of the day.

As I go along on this path of grief, I am realizing that this is going to be a common occurrence. It is something I do not look forward to but I know it is going to happen. I know it is going to happen no matter if I want it to or not and when this starts to happen, I let myself know not to worry. I tell myself I will make it through and that this is nothing new to me. The thing I hate about the whirlpool experience besides the feeling of being out of control is the loneliness of that place and the darkness, and empty feeling that goes with it. That is why I write. I write first, to help myself through that place and secondly, through my writing about it, I hope it will help others feel like they are not alone in the experience.

We who have lost children can never explain to others who have not lost their children to death what this feels like. We do not walk around with signs on our backs or black armbands like years ago. We walk in the world unnoticed by the people walking by. We walk in a world of our very own. A world no one would choose to walk in, if they had a choice. We live in a different world yet in the same world as everyone else. Somehow we have to bring the two worlds together and go on living in a world that no longer has a place for our children. We have to somehow live in a world where children are the hope of the future and live with the pain that ours are no longer a part of that world. Our hopes and dreams no longer can come from our children and that we have to find a place to put that hope. We have to find new hopes and dreams through ourselves and through others. We have to now refocus our energies for the positive not the negative and that my friend is hard to do when you are grieving your child. This is the place that either makes or breaks you as a person. To focus on the negative, could destroy us if we let it. We have to become new creations because we can never be the same again. A part of us died with our child.

A part of us will never grow. It will always stay the same and hold our child in that special place and we will go to that place often to hold our child and remember our child and be with them in a place no one can ever come. Surviving without our children will be a job we will have the rest of our lives. It will be a job with no days off. It will just be continuous movement forward and on some days backward. My hope for you, if you have lost a child, is that you know you are not alone. You are alone in your grief, but not alone in the experience. There are many of us in this world that walk by you every day that are in their own world full of pain and sorrow. They could even be behind that face that just smiled at you, you just never know. My goal in my writing is to share my experience in the everyday moments and tell it like it is. It may be raw and painful, or one of the better days when I see the so-called, bigger picture. I share it all, the good, the bad, and the ugly.

The Book That Never Ends

It seems that every time I try to end my book, I seem to be in another place in my process through grief. Each place seems different and most of the time a better place. I can feel myself growing all the time. My ba...ttle is trying to feel good as I process further down the road, without feeling guilty about where I am at. The way I move is by somehow putting my grief in a place that is shut off from the rest of my emotions. I have to tell myself this is what I am doing, then once I have done that, I have to give myself permission to go on and not only go on but to go on with the joy for living. I am learning how to do this and feel comfortable at the same time. I want to feel good in my skin and at peace with myself. I wish I didn't have to make a decision about how to do it, I wish I didn't have to think about it at all. For those of us that have to grieve our children we must know we will be doing this the rest of our lives. It is all about choices. We can choose to stay stuck in places in our grief or we can choose to move on. It is this choice that is so hard. The rest of the world would agree that this is the right choice. I can understand their reason for their thinking like that; Of course it is the better choice but not necessarily the easier one for the grieving parent. To those that love us and care about us it is the choice that says to them you are okay and getting on with your life. It is in these times that your grief becomes very personal and private. It is here where you can't share anymore. To share in this place with someone who hasn't been through this kind of grief is pointless. To them is seems like you are making a choice and the choice you are making is to hold on to the pain. How do you explain that to hold on to the pain is really your attempt to hold on to your child? And that the pain is just the catalyst to do that.

I am learning more about the pain every day. The feeling of pain changes all the time too, as you process through grief. The pain I felt in the beginning is different than the pain I feel today. The pain I feel today is more like a reminder, it serves as a gentle voice of my sub-conscious, letting me know or validating my experience. How do you tell the rest of the world that and if you did would they understand it? I think the biggest lesson I learned through my process through grief is this; in the beginning I wanted so much for everyone to understand me and my pain. I worked over time trying to get them to understand me. Why I did that I don't know. Now, as I look back I see I wasted a lot of energy trying to get them to understand me. It really isn't important for them to understand my pain. It is more important for me to understand why I needed them too. I think the hardest thing was hearing people say, you have to go on. God that use to get me so crazy! Of course I have to go on! And I choose that every day I decide to get out of bed and start my day. Going on is really the easy part. You just get up and go. You don't even think about it, you just do it. I am coming to an understanding I never thought I would and that understanding is: that sooner or later you just can't write enough about it and because grief is a process, a process that continues all the time. There really is no end to a grief book. It is a choice you make. You have to choose to stop writing, but just because you stopped writing, doesn't mean the process has ended, it just ended up to this point. The grieving parent is in reality a walking talking grief book and there is no ending to their book just different chapters written on the tablet of their heart and soul that will gently push them forward in a world without their child.

With love always
Liz Carthy